AMAZING RESUMES

What Employers Want to See—
and How to Say It

Jim Bright, Ph.D.

and

Joanne Earl, Ph.D.

JIST Works
America's Career Publisher

Amazing Resumes

Published in 2006 by JIST Works, an imprint of JIST Publishing, Inc.
8902 Otis Avenue
Indianapolis, IN 46216-1033
Phone: 1-800-648-JIST   Fax: 1-800-JIST-FAX   E-mail: info@jist.com

© Jim Bright and Joanne Earl, 2004, First Published by Allen & Unwin Australia

Visit our Web site at **www.jist.com** for information on JIST, free job search tips, book chapters, and ordering instructions for our many products! For free information on 14,000 job titles, visit **www.careeroink.com**.

Quantity discounts are available for JIST books. Please call our Sales Department at 1-800-648-5478 for a free catalog and more information.

Acquisitions and Development Editor: Lori Cates Hand
Interior and Cover Designer: Nick Anderson
Page Layout: Troy Barnes
Proofreader: Linda Seifert
Indexer: Kelly D. Henthorne
Printed in the United States of America
09 08 07 06 05   9 8 7 6 5 4 3 2 1
Library of Congress Cataloging-in-Publication data is on file with the Library of Congress.

ISBN 1-59357-182-8

Contents

Dedication

For Karen, William, Ben, and Graeme

Acknowledgments

There are many organizational psychologists, human resource managers, and recruitment consultants who have provided us with great assistance in writing this book. We would like to thank Fiona Davies, Prue Laurence, Sonia Hutton Manser, Dimitra Papadolias, Sharon Wilkenfeld, Lucy Harpham, Emma Lee, Lynne Clune, and Erin Stephenson, whose masters and honors research on resumes has provided us with invaluable help. Robert Bright was the human resources expert who started this all off—characteristically, over a curry dinner—with the simple question: What do we really know for sure about resumes? Jenny Reddin and Kodak Pty. Ltd. backed our early work. Our research was supported tremendously by Dr. Rob Anderson, Rachel Kenny, and Jennifer Blake. Special thanks to Ms. Doreen Cheong, who has guided our thinking on electronic resumes and co-presented seminars on this topic with us. Kevin Chandler from Chandler and Macleod Pty. Ltd. assisted us with the research on photographs and Web-based recruitment.

Many human resource professionals in Sydney and Melbourne assisted us by participating in our studies and reading through all the different resumes. Thanks to all our colleagues who have encouraged us in this project by reviewing our journal articles and even awarding us prizes! The School of Psychology at the University of New South Wales (UNSW) has supported these studies, and many of the staff there have provided useful feedback to us on the processes. Thanks to our collaborator Dr. Austin Adams for his generous help. Thanks to Tim Edwards for developing the original project. Thanks also to Emma Singer and Rachael Stock for their help in developing this book further. Finally thanks to Lori Cates Hand and all the excellent folks at JIST for believing in us, for having vision, for having enthusiasm, and for having the expertise to make this book what it is. Any shortcomings that may remain reflect the humble limitations of the authors.

Finally, thanks to Karen, Jim's life and business partner, who has taken these ideas, put them into practice, and developed them into a very successful career management business—Bright and Associates.

About the Authors

Jim Bright (B.A., Ph.D., MAPS, CPsychol, MAACC) is a leading and multiple-award-winning International Career Management expert who is a member of the National Career Development Association. He is an international bestselling author who has published seven books on career management, including *Brilliant CV* (the UK edition of this book); *Job Hunting for Dummies* (Australia); *Stress: Myth, Theory and Research;* and *Should I Stay or Should I Go? How To Make that Crucial Job Move Decision.* His books have been translated into five languages. A psychologist by training, Jim has trained literally thousands of professionals in the area of careers. He is an in-demand and entertaining trainer and speaker who has trained professionals in America, Australia, Europe, and Asia. Jim regularly appears on television, on the radio, and in national and international newspapers as a careers expert. He is a partner in a career management firm, Bright and Associates (www.brightandassociates.com.au), where his clients include individuals and many national and international organizations around the world. Jim has taught and researched career development at the School of Psychology at the University of New South Wales for a decade. He has published 50 peer-reviewed journal articles, chapters, and reports in leading national and international scientific journals on careers. Jim is married with two young sons—William and Benjamin—two cats, and two Welsh Springer Spaniels. In his spare time, he enjoys jazz music and sailing.

Joanne Earl (B.Ed., B.A., M.Psych [Applied], Ph.D., MAPS, AACC) was born in Adelaide, South Australia. She is a registered psychologist, a Member of the Australian Psychological Society (APS), a Member of the APS College of Organisational Psychology, and a member of the Australian Association of Career Counsellors. She has more than 15 years of experience working in business in various human resources, training, and psychological consulting roles. Passionate about learning, she continues to combine work and research. She is currently a senior consultant with the U.S. firm Gallup.

Introduction

Remember your first date, or the first time you went out with your partner? Did you make sure your clothes were right, your hair looked great, and you were wearing the right perfume or aftershave? Well, at least that much effort should go into getting your resume right! Resumes are "first dates" in the selection process that could land you on a new career path. Like the first date, they are the first time an employer has a chance to form an opinion about you—and first impressions can make all the difference.

Employers routinely get hundreds, if not thousands of resumes from candidates seeking the same job. That can mean odds of a thousand to one or even worse. A bad resume can reduce those chances from a long shot of a thousand to one to zero. A well thought-out resume can boost the same candidate's chance of being interviewed to one in three. Think about it: Just by changing your resume, you can go from a situation where no one would interview you to getting interviewed on every third occasion. In some cases we are able to boost a resume so that the candidate is always interviewed.

In our experience with career-transition clients, they tend to focus their nervous energy on the interview. Perhaps because the interview is closer to the final decision point, people think it is more important. However, it turns out that the interview is no more important than the resume in predicting the final decision. We have recently compared the importance of the resume with the interview in determining overall candidate suitability. The resume provides most data on competencies and achievements (or it should if it is properly written), whereas the interview provides more data on interpersonal skills and rapport. Resumes count! You must put as much effort into your resume as you do into your interview.

Getting a job today can involve several steps, starting with a resume, followed by psychological tests and interviews. The resume is the only step where you have full control over the information that you present. In every other step, the employer decides what questions to ask and what information to collect. The resume is your vital opportunity to present yourself at your best. Resumes are important.

There are many different books on the market providing advice on resume preparation. However, this is the first book that provides clear, down-to-earth advice that has been shown scientifically to work. This book is the culmination of years of dedicated scientific research into what makes a winning (and losing) resume.

We have interviewed hundreds of recruiters across a wide spectrum of industries and asked them to judge real resumes. The advice we now pass on to you is based on sound principles that have emerged from this work, and not on gossip, hearsay, or anecdotes. The aim of this guide is to provide you with no-nonsense advice about how to get the most out of your resume. It will increase your chances of being selected to be interviewed for that all-important job.

We show you how to put together a persuasive resume. We give examples of resumes that work and those that don't, and we explain to you why one works and another doesn't. We introduce you to some key job-seeking skills that will improve the quality of your resume. Every person has different strengths and weaknesses. The authors are organizational psychologists who understand these differences. Using simple exercises, we will show you how to tailor a resume to your own particular strengths.

In the following chapters we provide advice on the layout, content, and construction of your resume and its cover letter. We also address some of the tricky questions, like the following:

- Should I explain gaps in my career history?
- Do I need different resumes for different jobs?
- Should I describe all my duties at work?
- Can I e-mail my resume?
- Can I get any clues from the job advertisement that will improve my resume?
- Should I include a photograph?
- Can I leave stuff out of my resume and, if so, what stuff?
- How do I get my resume online?

We are confident that this guide will assist you in producing the best possible resume. The recruitment industry has assisted us in all of our work, and the advice we pass on here is a reflection of our close relationship with the people who are making decisions about resumes every day. The results of our work have been published in several industry and international scientific journals, and have been presented at international conferences in Australia and the United States. Training courses based on our work have been conducted in blue-chip companies.

How to Use This Book

This book is divided into four parts:

- Part 1 introduces the concept of a resume as a marketing document, and leads you through a series of exercises to help you put together a thorough resume.
- Part 2 builds on this by showing you how to enhance your resume to make it even stronger.
- Part 3 provides answers to some of those tricky questions regarding what to include and what to leave out, as well as issues such as references, cover letters, and dealing with prejudice. It also gives you an inside look at the recruiter's thought processes during selection. It also includes advice on how to address selection criteria, and a series of "before" and "after" resumes that will prove an invaluable resource when it comes to preparing your own resumes at any stage of your career.
- Part 4 provides some advice on using the Internet to find the right job, as well as a guide to putting your own resume online.

Throughout this book you will see "tips." All of these tips come straight from the human resource experts we interviewed and surveyed in our research program, so you know exactly what the experts want to see! Throughout the book, and in the last section especially, you will see graphs, figures, and tables that report data that have come straight from our studies, so at all times you are getting advice and the facts to back it up!

The first part of this book is designed to take you through some of the fundamental stages of putting together your resume. It will be particularly useful for readers who have never attempted to develop a resume before, or for those who have not done so recently. Of course, even if you already have a resume, it never hurts to revisit the basics to ensure that you are building from a strong foundation.

How to Sell Yourself

➤ *In this chapter you will learn how to*
- *Make your resume a sales and marketing document.*
- *Sell yourself as the "best buy" to an employer through your resume.*

Andy Warhol said everybody gets their 15 minutes of fame. Your resume is your opportunity to be in the spotlight; but unfortunately, most candidates are lucky to get five minutes. It depends on the job and the number of applicants, but hiring managers and human resource personnel will, on average, spend less than two minutes reading a resume. They'll never admit it publicly, but it is not unheard of for a manager to send a resume straight to the wastepaper basket after nothing more than a quick glance. Your job is to make the most of that tiny window of opportunity to sell yourself to the employer. Your resume must sell, sell, sell! It must sell *you*.

➤ **Tip:** Remember that you are marketing yourself; so while the integrity of the document is a must, the resume must present your best experience and detail your relevant skills and competencies.

Standing Tall: Presenting Yourself Positively

Some people become shy and retiring when we tell them to present themselves at their best. For many people, it is not natural to be forthcoming and assertive. Our language is filled with words and phrases that reflect this concern: "braggart," "blowing your own horn," "bighead," "showoff"! However, the fact of the matter is, you do have to sell yourself. Don't think that employers will run to your door, overcome and enchanted by your modesty and understatement. Still not convinced? Just consider all the other applicants. Will they be equally timid? You have to make your resume better than theirs. You have to make yourself better than them. Hands up, how many of you are thinking: "Oh no, I'm being asked to go way over the top, and that's not me!"? Remember, there are even more ways of selling things than there are ways of skinning cats (and most of them are a lot less noisy).

➤ **Tip:** Don't lay out your life, warts and all, and expect a recruiter to be able to pick through your story, see your inherent skills, and marvel at your honesty.

Consider the following three approaches to your resume:

Not Selling Yourself—Too Negative

> I did not enjoy college so I dropped out and traveled around for a couple of years. I got to see a lot of different countries, but eventually returned home, and I am now seeking a job....

Good Selling—Turning Negatives into Believable Positives

> After enrolling at college, I was provided with an opportunity to join a crew sailing around the world. I accepted this once-in-a-lifetime challenge, which offered me invaluable lessons in the importance of teamwork, shared responsibility, and leadership. I am now seeking to apply these skills....

Bad Selling—Over the Top, Unbelievable, and Undesirable

> I found I was not sufficiently challenged by the intellectual rigor of college life and left to pursue more appropriate ventures. I masterminded a round-the-world yacht race, and although there were other crew on board, most would probably agree I was the leader. I can now do wonders for you....

The purpose of checking these three approaches against your resume is to make the point that you should not confuse selling yourself with telling lies, wild exaggeration, or deliberately misleading someone. Selling yourself is about being positive and persuading others to share this view of you.

Suppose you are driving with a friend as passenger. He is getting impatient and wants to know when you'll arrive at your destination. You are halfway there. What do you say to soothe him? If the journey were two miles, then saying "Only another mile to go" would sound better than "We're only halfway there." If the journey were 1,000 miles in total, which would sound better: "Only another 500 miles to go," or "We're halfway there already"? Neither statement is untrue, nor misleading, but one serves your purposes well and the other does not. It is the same with resume writing.

➤ **Tip:** If you cannot say something in a positive way, consider not saying it at all.

But How Positive?

So selling is important. That said, remember that selling is like perfume—a little used judiciously is attractive and enhances the person, but drown yourself in perfume and it can be a big turnoff! The same goes for selling yourself: You need to know when to stop.

The following chapters go into detail about how best to sell yourself, but before we move on, test yourself with our "Over-the-Top" quiz.

Over-the-Top Quiz

Rate each of the following resume presentation ideas using this scale:
1. The work of a sad and deranged mind.
2. Not me, but I know someone who would.
3. Hmmm, sounds interesting; tell me more.
4. Who gave you a copy of my resume?

Make your resume stand out by using brightly colored paper and a really wacky font.	1 2 3 4
Have your resume delivered by a bikini-clad woman.	1 2 3 4
If you are a bank manager, set up your resume like a checkbook.	1 2 3 4
If you are an architect, design your resume in 3D, in the form of a house.	1 2 3 4
If you're going for a job in advertising, attach a condom to your resume ("I'm a SAFE bet...").	1 2 3 4

Now add up your points and check your score. How did you do?

4–5 points	You will lead a long, happy, and successful life. You were not tempted by these over-the-top ways of getting an employer's attention. These approaches nearly always fail, despite any rumors to the contrary you may have heard.
6–10 points	You are not a bad person, but you have some strange friends or are easily led. It's good to see you would not use these methods, but you could offer to rewrite the resumes of those who might be tempted.
11 points	Get help urgently! The help you need can be found in the section on wacky resumes. Read it carefully and follow the advice!
16–20 points	To quote from *Monty Python's Life of Brian:* "It is people like you wot cause unrest." Read the following section carefully and, for the sake of your job application, trust us: The wacky way is not the successful way!

The Wacky Resume

We have seen and heard of plenty of different "way-out" resumes and, without exception, we would never recommend them. Don't be tempted—not even for a minute. Some of you might be saying "Well, what's wrong with that idea?", or possibly "But you haven't read *my* resume!" Let's look at each in turn.

A Resume Delivered by a Bikini-Clad Woman

If you were going for a job as doorman at the Playboy Club circa 1975, this might have been a good move. Come on! Anyone using a semi-clad woman to advance his application will probably be written off as insensitive and coarse at best, and as a misogynist and a chauvinist at worst. Questions of appropriateness and targeting the particular requirements of the position are discussed later.

Bank Manager's Resume Set Up Like a Checkbook

When has being a raging individualist been a prerequisite for working in a bank? A recruiter might ask him- or herself why a bank manager needs to use gimmicks—what are they hiding? (And how would I get it in the photocopier?)

Architect's 3D Resume in the Form of a House

This is a bit more understandable, but again the candidate is risking appearing a bit cutesy or lightweight. And, of course, there are practical problems for recruiters receiving these sorts of resumes. How do they file or copy them easily?

Advertising Candidate Resume with Condom Attached

Please!

Using Colored Paper or Unusual Fonts

In a study we conducted with employers, all of them hated the unusual resume we showed them—it was on colored paper and printed in a strange font. When we presented the same resume on white paper in a standard font, all the employers were impressed. You will hear stories of people getting interviews and jobs that they think they got by using gimmicky resumes. These are exceptional cases—do not be tempted.

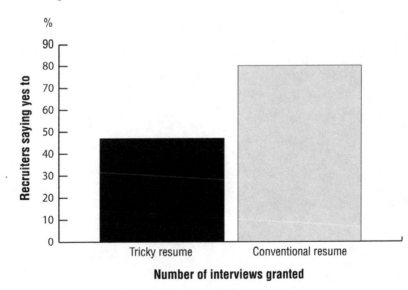

Figure 1.1: Recruiters' responses to unusual resumes.

➤ **Tip:** Never be tempted to use an unusual layout, no matter what success stories you hear.

Taste Test

So why do recruiters dislike "wacky" resumes? The answers could fill another book, but there are some examples in life that reinforce this view. Firstly, there is simple good taste. A painting by Picasso may be a great work of art to one person, and worse than a child's scribble to another. People's tastes differ. Many people tend to like things that are familiar. They also find them more memorable. It's sobering to realize that if you ask most Americans to name an artist, they are likely to say "Thomas Kinkade."

Secondly, people's opinions differ. Just think about music and sports. Some people think Pearl Jam is really cool, whereas others will always think Elvis is the King. Think about the arguments that rage about the NBA and NFL drafts. How does all this relate to resumes? All we are saying here is that things that are unusual will attract attention—like a Picasso painting or an unusual draft pick—and in return will elicit a reaction, positive or negative. If you don't know how the reader will react, why run the risk of rejection unnecessarily?

The Applicant-Employer Fit

> **In this chapter, you will learn**
> - How recruiters try to match resumes and jobs
> - How knowledge, skills, abilities, and attitudes are used to fit people to jobs.

What Is Fit?

If you hang around with recruitment consultants for long enough (about two minutes is usually enough), you will hear them talking about "fit." The way they see recruitment and the way many firms think about it is in terms of getting a good "fit" between the employer and the employee. Figure 2.1 illustrates this concept of fit.

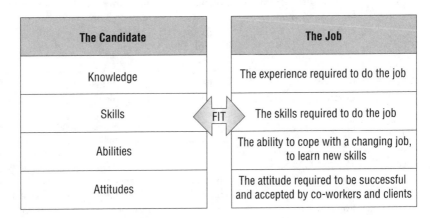

The Candidate		The Job
Knowledge		The experience required to do the job
Skills	FIT	The skills required to do the job
Abilities		The ability to cope with a changing job, to learn new skills
Attitudes		The attitude required to be successful and accepted by co-workers and clients

Figure 2.1: Factors in finding the right fit.

As you can see from the figure, fit is all about matching a candidate to a particular job. The best candidate for the job will be the one that best matches all the requirements of the job. You can see from Figure 2.1 that employers tend to think about "fit" in terms of four different qualities:

1. **Knowledge,** which refers to the experience and qualifications you possess.
2. **Skills,** which refers to the skills you have demonstrated (perhaps evidenced by your qualifications).
3. **Abilities,** which show your potential to carry out a range of different tasks beyond your immediate skills or knowledge, and the degree to which you can take on new tasks successfully or be trained in new methods or equipment.
4. **Attitudes,** which indicate your personality, and the degree to which you are enthusiastic, flexible, and positive in approach.

It is clear when you look at Figure 2.1 that merely putting your life history on a resume is highly unlikely to demonstrate the best fit. This is why it is so important to tailor your resume to the particular position—to increase the fit between you and the job.

The example in Table 2.1 illustrates this point. Three candidates have applied for a sales job. From reading their resumes, the employer has listed each candidate's knowledge, skills, abilities, and attitude on a grid, next to the job requirements. Which candidate fits the job best?

Table 2.1: Applicants for a Sales Assistant Job in a Drugstore

	Job Requirements	Kim	Liz	Jane
Knowledge	To know how a cash register works To know procedures for dealing with customers	Degree in English, worked part-time in a burger joint for 18 months	Worked in father's hardware store for 10 years	Worked in a shoe store for three years
Skills	Numeracy Good communication skills	Easily able to handle cash and card transactions	Easily able to handle cash and card transactions	Easily able to handle cash and card transactions
Abilities	To learn to process charge cards, electronic transactions	No difficulties learning new skills	No evidence of learning new skills	Probably able to deal with new payment methods with some training

continued

continued

	Job Requirements	Kim	Liz	Jane
Attitude	Polite, punctual, trustworthy, calm	Strong-minded, self-confident, assertive	Honest, a bit aloof at times	Calm, honest, level-headed
Degree of fit		Poor	Average	Good

We think that Kim is the weakest candidate. He has the best academic qualifications, but these are not necessary for the position offered. Although Kim could easily learn new skills and adapt to changing demands in the job, the comment in Kim's resume—"strong-minded person who is not afraid to stand my ground in disputes"—gives an unfortunate impression of someone who might be argumentative with the public.

Liz clearly has a lot of experience in the retail field, but in a very different area. There could be some concern about her ability to deal with customers sensitively. There does not appear to be much development of new skills over 10 years, and there is little evidence that she would adapt to new payment processes easily.

Jane looks like the strongest candidate to us. She has the necessary experience, and should be able to adapt to most new processes with training. She is not over- or under-qualified for the job and seems to be the best prospect.

In this analysis, you might think we have been terribly unfair to one or other of the candidates. Perhaps we have, but the point of this exercise is to illustrate the sorts of processes that recruiters go through when deciding to put applicants on their "shortlist" of preferred candidates.

Improving the Fit

When you write down job requirements as clearly as this, it is easy to see how you can start to mold your resume to match the job. Each of the candidates in Table 2.1 could probably have made themselves look the best by altering their resume. In this section we offer some advice; we describe these changes in more detail in the following chapters.

Kim could turn that negative remark about standing his ground into a positive by rephrasing it: "Confident person who enjoys talking to customers and helping them reach the right decision." Also, Kim could put more emphasis on his retail experience and less on his education. Perhaps a "career objective" statement outlining what Kim hopes to achieve would help persuade the recruiter that this is a serious career move for him. See Chapter 12 for more on how to write and use career objective statements.

Liz needs to make far more of her 10 years of experience. There must be many achievements and new skills she has learned. These need to be emphasized on the resume. Jane looks pretty good already, but perhaps she could try to emphasize her abilities, or her potential to learn more, by providing examples of new skills she has learned over the past three years.

So now you've seen that resumes need to sell, and you know how employers use the best "fit" as a guide to the best candidate. The next chapter shows you how to figure out what employers are looking for—how to determine the job's requirements.

➤ **Tip:** Make sure your resume addresses the advertised position.

Who Is the "Prime Suspect" for the Job You Want?

> **In this chapter, you will learn to**
> - Become a job detective
> - Find out as much as you can about a job before applying
> - Understand what an employer is looking for

Becoming a Job Detective

Imagine the scene: an office in the city, but there is someone missing from one desk. Witnesses say the missing person is dynamic, well qualified, and pays exceptional attention to detail. Every employer has a "prime suspect" in mind when they advertise a position, and they tend to leave clues to that person's identity in their job descriptions. In this chapter, we teach you to become a job detective, so that you can pick up all the clues and solve the mystery—what would the ideal candidate for this job look like?

To produce the best "fitting" resume, you need to know about yourself and you need to know about the job you are applying for. This chapter shows you how to figure out exactly what the job is all about. The following chapters then show you how to find out about yourself and best mold your resume to the job to produce the best fit.

> **Tip:** Resumes should always be written with the particular job in mind.

Job Detectives Question Themselves

Before you do anything else, ask yourself why you are preparing a resume. The answer to this question is going to vary from one person to the next, and here are our top 10 reasons for writing a resume:

1. You have seen a job advertised in the paper that appeals to you.
2. You want to market yourself to win a contract or a proposal, or be elected to a committee or organization.
3. You have seen a job on an Internet job site that appeals to you.
4. Your friends or family told you of a job opening at Earl and Bright, Inc.
5. You want to work for Earl and Bright, Inc., and thought that sending a resume to them might get their attention.
6. You have seen a job advertised internally at work.
7. You are going for a promotion.
8. You are about to be downsized and want to update your resume to be ready for any good opportunities.
9. You are feeling fed up and writing down all your achievements will cheer you up and might motivate you to look for a better job.
10. You are thinking "oh, so that's a resume! I've never done one. I suppose I ought to try to remember what I've been doing with my life!"

All of these certainly are good reasons to write a resume, but the resume serves many different purposes. One way of seeing the differences is to ask yourself who is going to read the resume in each case.

Resumes 1 to 5 will be read by potential employers who probably do not know you. Resumes 6 and 7 are likely to be read by your boss or other people who know you. Resumes 8 to 10 are really for your own benefit and should not be considered as suitable for sending out to employers.

The Right Mix

Think about the list of reasons again. How else can you divide up these reasons? A most important difference is that, in some cases, you will have a good idea of what the employer is looking for because you have a job advertisement in front of you and can tailor your resume accordingly. For others, you have no idea what the reader might want to see.

It is always worth updating your resume from time to time so you do not forget important details, but remember that the result of such a process will not be a winning resume. It will be a useful list of tasks and achievements.

Writing a resumes is like baking a cake. You need all the right ingredients: flour, butter, eggs, and so on. It is what you do with the ingredients that makes the difference between a great resume (or cake) and failure. Keeping your resume up-to-date is like keeping a stock of ingredients in the pantry—it's potentially very useful, but do not imagine that is the end of it!

If there is a most important piece of advice we can give you, it is that you must think about what the employer is looking for and then reflect it in your resume. This advice was the most common tip from a large sample of hiring managers.

> **Tip:** Think about what the employer is looking for and then reflect that in your resume.

Getting Information About the Job and the Company

You should tailor the information in your resume to the main points in the job advertisement. That sounds fine, but how do you do it? Get as much information about the job and the company as you can. When you've gotten that, go and find some more!

Information About the Job

The main sources of information about a job are normally the following:

- A job advertisement
- A job description
- A friend in the company
- The media
- Gossip and rumor
- Someone already doing the job or something similar

There is no substitute for experience. Talking to someone who does a job similar to the one you wish to apply for in the same company may well provide you with a good picture of what the job is really like. Bear in mind, of course, that this source of information is not always reliable. You may react differently than the way that person does, and therefore their experience with a company may be very different than yours.

However, someone with reliable information can provide a golden opportunity. Make sure you do not waste the chance to get some information. One way of ensuring that the information you get is useful is to use the job advertisement interrogation questions in the next chapter.

> **Tip:** The best published source of information about what specific jobs are like is the *Occupational Outlook Handbook*, by the U.S. Department of Labor. It gives details on more than 270 job titles held by 88 percent of the U.S. workforce. To access this information online, go to www.bls.gov/oco.

Information About the Company

The main sources of information about an employer are normally the following:

- The media
- Annual reports/company brochures
- Industry/trade magazines or journals, such as *Fortune* magazine
- The Internet—on the company's own site or at general sites such as Hoovers Online (www.hoovers.com)
- Industry directories
- Gossip and rumor

There are many other sources of information about companies; and, if you're serious about wanting to know more about a potential employer (and you should be), it's also worth a visit to your local library. Ask a reference librarian to help you with your search. It will help if you explain to the librarian that you are looking for information on a specific company to help with your job search.

Understanding an Employer's WIIFT

When thinking about any employer, you should always keep in mind how they will see you and what benefits they may see in hiring you. This is known in the trade as the "WIIFT," or "What's In It For Them?" Understanding the company helps you to better understand the WIIFT—that is, the benefits of having you as an employee. Later chapters go into detail about how to use your resume to show employers "what's in it for them."

➤ **Tip:** Do your homework prior to applying for a job. Find out about the company, and obtain an annual report if they have one. Find out what future projects the company might be involved with, and who their clients and competitors are.

How to Read
a Job Ad

➤ **In this chapter, you will learn**
  - *How to take the right information from a job advertisement*
  - *How to find out what the company does and what they want from you*
  - *What personal qualities are needed to get the job*

The Job Detective Examines the Job Advertisement

Job advertisements and descriptions should be treated as clues. Job advertisements are usually reliable sources of information that you can take seriously. Employers can be found to have broken the law if they put misleading or incorrect information in advertisements.

Information from other sources can sometimes be invaluable, but sometimes it can be grossly inaccurate. The same principles apply whatever the source of the information.

On the following page is a typical job ad. Below it are our tips for reading the ad. After reading the job ad, use the seven questions that follow it to assist in breaking down the job ad successfully. Remember, reading an ad properly is the crucial first step in preparing a successful resume.

Training Manager
Nerck Pharmaceuticals

Would you like to join the world's third biggest pharmaceutical company, currently expanding rapidly in the Midwest U.S. market? We require a manager to join our training division, where you would be responsible for the delivery of training programs to our sales staff. A dynamic, results-focused team player, you will have excellent communications skills, and will be able to handle pressure and work to deadlines. With several years of solid experience in an international company, you will be accredited in NLP and will have a basic understanding of training evaluation techniques. Reporting to our Regional Manager, you will be required to provide input into the marketing strategies for the Midwest region by training our sales staff to improve market share.

Please forward your resume to: Jim Price, Personnel Dept., Nerck Pharmaceuticals, 5800 Washington Street, Evansville, IN 47715; or jprice@nerck.com.

EOE/AA

The Seven Job Advertisement Interrogation Questions

1. What don't you understand about the job ad?
2. What type of industry/company is it? What's happening in the company or industry? Is it restructuring or expanding? Does it operate with low overheads and high profit margins?
3. What is the main purpose of the job being offered?
4. Why is this job important to the company? How will this job affect the company's bottom line?
5. What types of skills does the company want? What other skills might be needed, given the job's purpose?
6. What types of personal qualities does the company want? What other personal qualities might be needed, given the job's purpose?
7. What types of knowledge/training does the company want? What other knowledge or training might be needed, given the job's purpose?

An Explanation of Each Interrogation Question

Now that you have read the questions, we will take you through them one at a time.

1. What Don't You Understand About the Job?

Here are some definitions to help you understand our example.

EOE stands for Equal Opportunity Employer, and AA (Affirmative Action) refers to companies that have policies of non-discrimination in the workforce on the basis of gender, ethnicity, sexual preference, age, or other factors. Affirmative Action programs are those that recognize the difficulties of particular disadvantaged groups' experience in the workforce and take steps to promote their interests.

Neurolinguistic programming (NLP) is a controversial training technique that is intended to improve both verbal and non-verbal communication.

A general clue to the significance of these jargon terms can be gleaned from their positions in the ad. If the jargon words appear next to descriptions of qualifications required, it is a good bet that the words refer to skills you will need (such as NLP, in this case). If the words appear toward the end of the ad where the contact details appear, or near a description of the company, then it is likely that these words refer to general conditions of employment or company policy (such as EOE/AA).

If you are still stuck, you could try contacting the Department of Labor about the phrases that may have legal meanings, like EOE. You could always contact the employer and ask; but if you think this may create a poor impression, find a friend to call instead.

If the terms are likely to refer to a technical aspect of the job, it may be worth visiting your library and searching for books on the subject, or contacting the relevant professional association or trade union (such as the Associated General Contractors of America, the American Institute of Certified Public Accountants, or the Society of American Foresters).

In addition to standard reference works like dictionaries, thesauruses, and encyclopedias, logging on to the Internet is a very powerful way to search for information. If you use the Internet, you can search for a particular keyword or phrase that you do not understand. Another good idea would be to try out some of the job websites we recommend in Part 4. These contain explanations of work-related terms, and some carry profiles of different employers and company sections.

2. What Type of Industry or Company Is It and What's Happening Currently?

You can glean some of this information from the job ad. In our example, the company seems to operate on a global scale because it asks for experience in international companies. Secondly, it gives the impression it is expanding in that part of the world. However, that doesn't mean that it is expanding everywhere, and it doesn't say the job will be located in Indiana, where the correspondence address happens to be. The job may involve overseas travel, or be based overseas. It is not possible to tell whether the company is restructuring or what its profitability is.

Information about companies can be gleaned from many different sources. Remember our earlier tip to visit your local library to review any existing information in such publications as *Fortune* magazine. Ask a librarian how best to conduct your search. It is easy to miss huge chunks of information.

Do you know anyone who works for the company? If so, talk to them. Could they get ahold of any company brochures, newsletters, or other advertising material for you? In our example, you might ask whether there is anything in the latest pharmaceutical trade journals.

If you are very interested in working for a large company, start reading the business pages of the newspaper to see if there are any stories about the company. If it is a public company, you can ask for a copy of the annual report. This may tell you whether the company is growing, how profitable it is, and whether any layoffs are planned.

Because this company sells pharmaceuticals, it might be worth going to a pharmacy to ask about the company, or asking a doctor. Then you might be able to find out whether this company sells medicinal products. Also check out the supermarkets to see whether this company sells domestic products such as laundry detergent. Take the job ad with you so you can match the logo and address with the products on the shelf.

3. What Is the Main Purpose of the Job?

In this case, it is fairly clear that the main duties will be to conduct training of sales staff. Duties are likely to be fairly well known by job applicants because the job requires somebody with experience and qualifications. However, training itself is a broad role that may involve many responsibilities. It may be that the company specializes in an industry that has very specific training needs. For example, a petroleum company may have to adhere to Occupational Safety and Health Administration (OSHA) requirements for using chemicals. Alternatively, training may involve stress-management techniques in a high-pressure work environment. It is well worth finding out what particular needs a company may have over and above those in the job advertisement.

4. Why Is This Job Important to the Company?

The job is important because the company wants to increase sales of its products. To do so, it thinks it needs better trained sales staff. The company will be looking for someone who can demonstrate an impact on sales through improved training.

5. What Types of Skills Does the Company Want and What Other Skills Might Be Needed?

The company wants someone who can teach NLP. Other than that, you will need to be able to gauge whether the company's training program is successful (evaluation). Good communication skills are also required. In this job, this involves being able to talk to groups of trainees, to produce clear training materials, and to be able to write reports and present them to management. Because the company is linking the job to strategic planning, it will be important that you are able to demonstrate general business and commercial awareness. Be sure you know your way around a balance sheet.

6. What Personal Qualities Does the Company Want and What Other Qualities Might Be Needed?

The company wants someone who is "dynamic"—meaning somebody who can motivate the sales staff and conduct interesting training courses, and generally make an enthusiastic addition to the staff. Communication and team player skills mean you need to get along well with others, speak well (in public), and write well.

7. What Knowledge and Training Does the Company Want and What Other Knowledge/Training Might Be Needed?

A degree in psychology, business, or commerce may be useful. Any evidence of business-related experience is probably very useful. Experience in a similar job would be good. The ability to speak a relevant language should improve your chances.

You can see already how, in answering these questions, we are building up a picture of the type of job that is being offered, and the sorts of qualities the candidate should possess. Therefore, we are increasing the chances of a good fit.

You Become the Job Detective

Following are a series of job advertisements. Read through each advertisement and make your own list of answers to the job interrogation questions, building your own picture of what the employer wants to see in a candidate. We have completed the first exercise for you.

Exercise 4.1: A Completed Example

Administrative Assistant

Due to expansion, an exciting opportunity exists for a person to assist the Administration Manager in a wide variety of work such as marketing mailings, customer relations, and all other aspects of administration. Applicants must possess good communication skills with the ability to work under pressure during peak work load times. Knowledge of Word and Excel essential. Package negotiable.

Send resume to:
Human Resources Director,
American Insurance Brokers
P.O. Box 86
Cleveland, OH 44101

Let's take a look at the job and examine it together.

1. What Don't You Understand About the Job?

"Knowledge of Word and Excel essential." This refers to the computer programs that you will need to know. Any job requiring significant typing or data-processing work will probably list the sort of computer programs you should be familiar with. The most common are Microsoft programs such as Word (a word-processing program) and Excel (a spreadsheet program). "Package negotiable" means that there is no set salary for the job. You will have to negotiate it with the employer and this negotiation may also include the number of hours worked, the retirement contributions, and other benefits.

2. What Type of Industry or Company Is It?

These insurance brokers are expanding, but it is not clear whether just this department is expanding or the whole company is expanding. A trip to the library to look up past issues of the *Wall Street Journal* or a local business journal such as *Crain's Cleveland Business* will help you to figure out what's happening with the company.

3. What Is the Main Purpose of the Job?

The main purpose of the job is administration—mail, maybe drafting correspondence, typing (using Word), filing, perhaps keeping schedules for managers, coordinating meetings, travel, maybe working with spreadsheets (in Excel), marketing mailings, and dealing with customers.

4. Why Is This Job Important to the Company?

The job is to assist the Administration Manager to process administration efficiently and effectively. Any company lives and dies on its efficiency, and without an effective administration system professionally run by competent staff, profits will be seriously affected. Your job is to help the administration manager make this system run smoothly.

5. What Types of Skills Do They Want?

Communication skills: You are likely to draft correspondence and will need to have good verbal communication to follow instructions. Time-management skills: Companies tend to run under time constraints, so time-management skills will help you be effective in your job. Organizational skills: To help organize the company's administration, you will need to be organized yourself! Customer relations: In this job you will be dealing with queries, coping with complaints, and managing problems the administration manager cannot deal with. You will need to be understanding, patient, and diplomatic.

6. What Types of Personal Qualities Do They Want?

This job is clearly a support role, so reliability, punctuality, good organizational skills, and attention to detail will all be highly regarded. Given that you are dealing with the public and have to work under pressure, somebody who is polite and not too hot-tempered would probably be a good fit.

7. What Types of Knowledge/Training Do They Want?

The critical training/knowledge here is in Word and Excel. Because the advertisement does not specify a level of expertise, it is reasonable to assume that you will need to be reasonably proficient in both. You will need to know what the programs do, how to produce standard documents in both packages, and how to print them out or otherwise present them. You might need to become very proficient in one or both of these programs.

Are You a Sherlock Holmes or an Inspector Clouseau?

Here is your chance to find out what sort of detective you are. All you have to do is analyze the following three advertisements (exercises 4.2, 4.3, and 4.4) using our seven job interrogation questions. You will find a blank worksheet with the seven questions below. Photocopy this to write down your answers and keep extra copies for when you do this with "real" advertisements of jobs you wish to apply for.

Use the approach we took in exercise 4.1 as a framework, and try to be as concise as possible without leaving out anything important. You can then compare your answers with the experts' answers that follow each ad. At the end, add up your scores to see how you did. Good luck!

My analysis is…

1. Check of terminology

   _____

   _____

2. Type of industry/company

   _____

   _____

3. Main purpose of the job

_____

_____

4. Importance of the job to the company

_____

_____

5. Skills wanted

_____

_____

6. Personal qualities wanted

_____

_____

7. Knowledge/training wanted

_____

_____

Exercise 4.2

Computer Analyst/Programmer

An outstanding opportunity exists to join our leading-edge software consulting firm as an Analyst Programmer using the latest client/server technology. We are looking for a creative and innovative thinker who has a strong desire to be the best they can be in an environment that offers vast opportunities and rewards to dedicated and determined staff. You will be working and/or be trained alongside some of the best software developers in the field. Experience in Visual Basic, Access, SQL Server, and Internet development with tertiary qualifications is very helpful. If you are ambitious and have an enthusiastic personality, you are ideal for these challenging and exciting jobs. Top salary and compensation, bonuses and incentives, with interstate and/or international travel opportunities for the right applicant/s. We are committed to the principles of equity and diversity.

Send resume to:
Human Resources Director,
Softly Softly Inc.
P.O. Box 6654
Detroit, MI 45038

The Experts' Analysis

1. Check of Terminology

Visual Basic, Access, and SQL Server are technical computing terms you need to look up and understand if you don't already. "Equity and diversity" refer to the company's policy to make sure it hires and promotes people of both genders and all ethnicities with equal consideration.

2. Type of Industry/Company

Software consulting firm.

3. Main Purpose of the Job

Software development using client/server technology. In this case, you would probably have to meet with clients and come up with solutions to their software problems. This would often involve writing special programs for the clients using the computer languages listed in the ad, such as Visual Basic or Access.

4. Importance of the Job in the Company

"Creative and innovative thinker"—the company is looking for someone who can think outside the box in developing new software products. In other words, you should be good at writing computer programs that can do the tasks required by the client. Your ability to deliver programs that not only work well but also address clients' needs is probably of central importance to the company.

5. Skills Required

Ability to develop new software products using Visual Basic, Access, SQL Server, and Internet programming languages.

6. Personal Qualities

Creative, innovative, ambitious, dedicated, determined (tenacious?), enthusiastic. All these personal qualities suggest somebody who is good at solving the problems that clients have. This may involve coming up with different solutions for every client instead of just trying to apply the same solution to every problem. This is the "innovative" and "creative" part. The need for dedication and determination suggests that you need to be able to see a problem through until it is solved and not give up too easily. "Enthusiasm" suggests that the company is looking for somebody who relishes problem-solving.

7. Knowledge/Training

The knowledge and training required are reasonably clearly stated. You must be able to use the computer programs they mention to a high standard. Tertiary qualifications seem to be valued, too.

Exercise 4.3

Sales Representatives

Deci Co. in Orlando requires Sales Representatives to expand their sales to corporate clients. While experience in the printing industry is not essential, a proven sales and service ability in the above market would be a clear advantage. You should be highly motivated and focused on building a client base. You understand that success comes from building relationships with customers and tenaciously developing and promoting printing solutions to a wide industry client base. This position suits a practical results-driven achiever who seeks an attractive compensation package.

Please send resume to:
Douglas Giles
Giles Recruitment
P.O. Box 22679
Orlando, FL 32876

The Experts' Analysis

1. Check of Terminology

There is little or no jargon here. The main issue would be to ensure that you understand what is meant by "corporate clients." (It probably means big business, but may just refer to the fact that you are selling to other companies and not to the public.)

2. Type of Industry/Company

Deci Co. Printing Products and Services. What services and products does this company offer? How can you find out? Call the company for a brochure. Look it up in the Yellow Pages. Search the Web—use the Web-based Yellow Pages and see what classification the company is listed under. Do you have any friends who might have some idea—people working in the business, or even people who work near the company's address in Orlando?

3. Main Purpose of the Job

Selling printing products and providing services to corporate clients. This will probably involve persuading clients to use your company to print all their brochures, stationery, or whatever else the company offers.

4. Importance of the Job in the Company

Expanding sales via building and servicing a new client base. The sales position is a crucial one for many companies because without clients there is no business.

5. Skills Required

The sorts of skills required will include the following:
- Selling skills—securing new clients
- Customer service—looking after existing clients
- Problem-solving—identifying opportunities for new clients

6. Personal Qualities

These will include highly motivated, tenacious, results-driven, and achievement-oriented. These skills are important because sales staff are often paid a high proportion of their salary as commission on the sales that they achieve. Consequently, you need to be the type of person who will go looking for new opportunities (motivated), be prepared to bounce back quickly when a client says "no" initially (tenacious), and have a need to achieve goals or meet sales targets (achievement-oriented).

7. Knowledge/Training

Knowledge of the printing industry would be useful because it means you will understand the products, services, and technology; know who your competitors are; know who the most likely good clients are; and so on. Knowledge of strategies to build a client base would also be extremely useful. This might involve a good existing network of contacts who may turn into future clients, or experience in building up a network of clients in a previous job.

Exercise 4.4

General Manager—Technology
Our client, a national leading retailer, is seeking a General Manager to lead its business in a period of strong growth here and overseas.

The job
Principally the job will focus on developing a strategic IT plan that supports business objectives and future system requirements. There is a need to review and evaluate existing hardware/software and to manage a small support team.

The person
You are a business manager first and foremost who understands the retail industry. You have a thorough understanding of information technology, including current and future directions across the Internet/Intranet and Extranet. You possess strong people-management skills and appreciate the importance of getting the best out of your staff. You have exceptional presentation skills and can tailor content to suit a broad audience. Excellent written presentation skills are required to communicate organizational needs and persuade senior management to implement system changes. This is an excellent opportunity for a successful individual to join a rapidly developing organization and to make an impact on its future direction.

Please send your resume to:
Claudia Joy
Claudia Joy Management Recruiting, Inc.
P.O. Box 3200
Kansas City, MO 63104

The Experts' Analysis

1. Check of Terminology

"IT" stands for Information Technology, which refers to electronic devices and systems that manage and share information, such as computers and networks, word processors, faxes, the Internet, e-mail, and even mobile phones. Internet, Intranet, and Extranet refer to the different systems that link computers together to share information either globally (Internet), within the company (Intranet), or within a company but extending to select others outside the company (Extranet).

2. Type of Industry/Company

Leading national retailer: the company sells products to consumers (and may possibly manufacture them, too).

3. Main Purpose of the Job

Managing the development and implementation of a strategic IT plan involves making sure the company has in place an IT system that can deal adequately with all the computing and communication needs of the company now and in the foreseeable future.

4. Importance of the Job in the Company

Providing IT solutions that are aligned with current business needs and anticipated future IT requirements is very important. There are some sorry tales around about companies having to scrap their new computer systems because they found them to be inadequate to do the job required of them. Of course, such blunders are not cheap to fix.

5. Skills Required

The sorts of skills required are the following:
- Leadership—implementing change
- Strategic business planning
- Decision-making
- People management—managing a small support team
- Performance management—keeping the team's performance at the appropriate level
- Presentation skills—oral and written.

6. Personal Qualities

A persuasive and decisive person would probably do well here. The emphasis is on being good at getting the rest of the team to work effectively and being good at making decisions. The last point may sound strange, but managers who are unable to decide between one of several options can cause tremendous problems at work, because while they are prevaricating, nothing productive gets done!

7. Knowledge/Training

The sorts of skills that would be useful include the following:
- Knowledge of the retail industry
- Business management
- IT (Internet, Intranet, Extranet)
- Ability to change management techniques

How Did You Score?

Now that you have analyzed the sample ads and compared your answers with those offered by our team of experts, you can find out how many points you've scored and assess how well you read the ads.

Give yourself two points each time your answer agrees with the experts. Total your score for each job ad and look up your score using the following chart.

Scoring Chart

0–8 points	Inspector Clouseau—Yikes! Best to go back and start again. Writing a resume that addresses only a couple of key points means it is likely to get thrown out with the rest. It may be the reason you've missed out on being put on the "short list" previously.
10–30 points	Dr. Watson—Still some work to do, but you're almost halfway there. What did you miss? Go back and check the sections you scored most poorly on.
32–42 points	Sherlock Holmes—Congratulations! The closer you scored to 42, the better chance you have of getting on the employer's short list. But be careful! In some cases, failing to identify the importance of some fundamentals such as industry knowledge can still result in an almost perfect resume being rejected.

If at this stage you were unable to answer some of the questions clearly, maybe you need extra information. The following chapters describe some of the sources of such information in more detail, so that you'll know what you should be looking for.

CHAPTER 5

Reading Job Descriptions

In this chapter, you will learn
- *What a job description looks like*
- *How to not be intimidated by the qualities that are apparently demanded by a job description*

Job descriptions are another very important source of information about a job. A job description is often provided when you contact a company asking for further details. Sometimes an employer will request that you pick up a job description before you apply for a job. Sometimes a job description will be on hand as part of the company's normal human resources documentation. In essence, it is a longer version of the job advertisement. Some job descriptions also go into greater detail about the company and its history. In analyzing job descriptions, you should ask the same seven questions that you did about the job advertisement.

A Sample Job Description

Here is a sample job description.

Job Description

Bright and Earl—The Cowboy's Bank

Home of the Horse Traders

At Bright and Earl, we are committed to providing our clients with brilliant service every day. We offer a full and competitive range of products. The exclusive Bright and Earl Horse Traders plan means that we will buck the

---

trend on poor performance of our competitors and give our customers exactly what they deserve. This means integrity, attention to detail, precision, and prompt service. There are no long faces in this stable!

If you can make a difference in our organization and have the attributes we desire, please saddle up and read about the outstanding opportunities within our company in Hungry Horse, Montana.

Information Security Project Manager

As an Information Security Project Manager with Bright and Earl, you will

- Be responsible for managing all activity for a software or security area. May be responsible for a larger project related to bank-wide IT security. Position manages a project staff of 10 to 20 employees. Projects are technically complex and require superior analytical skills. Projects are generally completed in 12 to 24 months and have a budget of $2 to $4 million.

- Direct and supervise project activity for an assigned functional area.

- Participate in meeting and bank activities to implement project goals, gain buy-in on project steps, plan and implementation procedures, and calculate project costs; create an atmosphere of cooperation and involvement with support team.

- Interview clients to identify and understand needs; plan project and provide recommendations for request and/or problem resolution.

- Utilize all appropriate internal and external resources to ensure successful and timely project completion.

- Prepare regular project status reports; be responsive to feedback and change project plan as needed.

- Assist with or prepare project implementation steps and documentation as appropriate; ensure a smooth implementation of project; resolve problems.

- Train users in new systems.

- Evaluate project against estimated plans and costs; provide continuing support and service as required.

- Manage performance of project team and evaluate overall performance.

We require:

- A comprehensive level of knowledge of assigned business functions and thorough technical skills.

- A bachelor's degree and five years of related experience; PMP essential; CISSP a plus.

Bright and Earl is committed to diversity. Please send your resume, including reference code Horse-Feathers , via e-mail, mail, or fax to the address or number listed below.

Searching for Even More Description

If a company is big enough, there may be information about it available in the media. This may be found in the business sections of papers or on the Internet. Sometimes a company will be in the papers for negative reasons such as labor strikes, injuries, or discrimination cases. While the media may give only a partial view of the company, you might get some really valuable information, too.

The Internet is a particularly important source of information. Many companies now have home pages on the Web that will tell you a lot about them. Company home pages can be searched for on the Web using standard search engines such as AltaVista, Yahoo!, Google, and Excite. When searching, try a variety of different keywords such as "AT&T" or "Telecommunications Companies." In Part Four, we provide a list of useful job-related links.

Many large-scale companies decide to subcontract their recruiting to specialist management consulting firms such as PricewaterhouseCoopers, Adecco, Management Recruiters International, and Snelling. These firms all have home pages, and within their pages there may well be links to their clients' home pages. Try looking on the Web pages of the companies that place recruitment advertisements (such as HotJobs and Monster).

The Internet a good tool for finding out where the job hunting action is. If you are serious about looking for work or applying for jobs, you have to get onto the Internet and check out what's available and how to apply. More information on using the Internet can be found in Part Four of this book.

Finally, there are always people out there happy to pass on their opinions with little regard to how accurate they may be. We've all met the sort: "Oh, I wouldn't work for them, they want your soul," or "The boss is a drunk—it's well known," or "They sell cigarettes to children." Try to get as much *objective* evidence as possible about prospective employers. If people pass on these sorts of comments, ask them to justify what they say, or where they heard it. If they cannot come up with anything more credible than "Everyone knows that!" or "A friend of my brother's," we suggest you disregard it.

They Must Want Superman!

Having read all these ads and job descriptions, you could be forgiven for thinking that companies are looking for extraordinary skills and abilities in their employees. It is only human nature—after all, if you were the employer, wouldn't you be looking for the best possible employees? However, do not be put off by the over-the-top language that is often used. Behind all the bluster you probably have all the qualities they are looking for.

➤ **Tip:** Job ads often sound as though they are looking for a superhuman candidate! Don't be too easily put off from applying. If you are not in the game, you cannot win it.

Remember that your aim, as a job detective analyzing job advertisements, is to try to figure out what the ideal candidate or "prime suspect" might look like. If the person you come up with could not possibly exist (no one is that perfect!) you have probably gone wrong somewhere. Go back and see where you might have exaggerated the required attributes, or where the employer might be being unrealistic.

When you have answered all of the job detective questions, you should have a much clearer picture of what it is that the company wants. Now you can form your plan of attack. The next chapter will get you started.

CHAPTER 6

Do You Fit the Job?

In this chapter, you will learn how to
- *Make a list of your career milestones*
- *Maximize your achievements*
- *Tailor your achievements to the job*

Applying for a job can be very competitive, especially if the company has a good reputation, or the position is particularly exciting—both things you are looking for in a new job. It doesn't pay to overestimate your skills beyond your abilities, but it also seriously disadvantages you if you are overly negative.

It constantly amazes recruiters when they receive, all too commonly, cover letters that begin: "Dear Sir, First of all can I point out that I don't have the required experience, but…" Of course, nobody likes to appear big-headed, and it can be hard to describe your own abilities and not feel this way. As Ernest Hemingway once said, "You see it's awfully hard to talk or write about your own stuff because if it is any good, you yourself know about how good it is—but if you say so yourself you feel like a [jerk]."

The point is that a potential employer wants to know what you can do, and playing down your genuine abilities will not represent you in an accurate light.

Who Are You?

Now that you've painted the picture of the ideal candidate in the preceding chapters, how do you go about listing your skills to prove how well you fit the job? Here are our tips to help you describe yourself.

When it comes to describing themselves, many people forget potentially vital details, or think that some achievements are probably irrelevant to their resume. Then again, there are some people who downplay their achievements. Finally, there are those people who just cannot see that "played on the Little League team" is not as important as "was elected President…"

In our research, we found that those candidate resumes that were focused on outcomes and achievements were more likely to be shortlisted by recruiters and hiring managers than resumes that described the duties and responsibilities of each previous job.

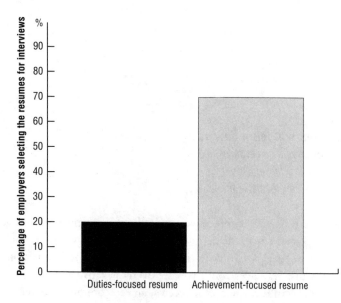

Figure 6.1: What is the most successful focus for your resume?

The four most common faults here are
- Forgetting some potentially impressive achievements
- Thinking some achievements are not relevant
- Playing down your achievements
- Including every boring, irrelevant detail

You're probably saying to yourself, "Hang on. They are telling me not to exclude relevant stuff and in the next breath they are saying do not include irrelevant material. That's really helpful!" We're about to introduce you to some exercises that will assist you in determining what is important and what is not.

Building a Personal History

First of all, you need a list of your past activities and your achievements. We suggest that to ensure you do not omit anything by accident, you should try to list your past in as much detail as possible. At this stage, do not attempt to decide whether the information is relevant.

We have developed some forms to help you get all the relevant details down in some order. Some people may find it easier to jot things down as they come to them, which is just fine. But you may wish to put all the information into our worksheets when you have finished. Divide your life into the sections, where applicable, listed in Table 6.1; then refer to the suggested worksheet to flesh out your details.

Table 6.1: Choosing Which Worksheets to Use

Stage of Life	Appropriate Worksheet
Secondary school (typically 14–18 years old)	Worksheet 1
Vocational training (16–22 years old)	Worksheet 1
College (usually 18–22 years old)	Worksheet 1
Any postgraduate training (typically in your 20s)	Worksheet 1
Jobs held in the first five years after completing your training/education (between 20 and 30 years)	Worksheet 2
Jobs held in your 30s	Worksheet 2
Jobs held in your 40s	Worksheet 2
Jobs held in your 50s and so on	Worksheet 2
Life achievements/awards/ community work/sports and hobbies	Worksheet 3

Of course, many career histories will vary from the one shown here. Here are a couple other models.

For people without formal education, try:

- Jobs held between 15 and 20
- Jobs held 20–30
- Jobs held 30–40
- Jobs held 40–50 and later

You should use Worksheets 2 and 3.

For people who joined the workforce later in life, try:

- What you did before starting training/joining the workforce
- Any training
- First five years of work
- Next 10 years
- The next 10 years, and so on

You should use all three worksheets, but it may be that Worksheet 3 (the Life worksheet) is the most important for you.

You can see that the general pattern we are suggesting here is to divide up your life into sections, which you might think of like this:

- Early work and training
- Early jobs post-training
- Mid-career jobs
- Later-career jobs

When you have settled on a way of dividing up your life that suits you, use our worksheets to guide the process. First we give you the blank worksheets. Then we give you an example of how someone might fill out each of them.

Worksheet 1: Training

High School _____

Dates Attended From _____   to _____

Subjects Studied	Grades

Teams or Clubs _____

Achievements

Worksheet 1: Training (Example)

High School   St. Joan of Arc

Dates Attended From   1979   to   1985

Subjects Studied	Grades
Latin	C
Home Economics	A
Sports	D
English	B
Math	C
Spanish	F
Geography	D
Teams or Clubs	Basketball club
Achievements	I played on the championship team of 1981. I captained the team in 1983 and we came in second out of 20 teams.

For each place where you had any training, complete the details. You should try to list the following:

- Any training you undertook
- The institution
- Everything you studied (the correct titles of the subjects)
- The grades you got in each subject
- Your overall grade-point average and any distinctions
- How that training was/could be useful to you in your work

It is worth mentioning here that one of the most frequent difficulties for people reading resumes is to figure out what exactly a particular qualification or result actually means. Have a look at what we have to say about this in Chapter 8.

Worksheet 2: Jobs

Employer Name and Address

Dates Attended: From _____ to _____

Reasons for leaving

Job Title	Dates	Key Duties	Achievements/ Promotions

Training Undertaken	Instructor/ Organization	Date	Description	What I Learned

---

Worksheet 2: Jobs (Example)

Employer Name and Address   Old Joe Pigtail and Associates, 2 Main Street, East St. Louis, IL

Dates Attended From   1987   to   1991

Reasons for leaving   To get broader experience with Mega Media International

Job Title	Dates	Key Duties	Achievements/ Promotions
Junior Accounts Consultant	1987–88	Assisting Accounts Consultant	I was the first employee to be promoted to Accounts Consultant within one year, and also the youngest person to have held that position in the company's history
		Analyzing sales figures	I redesigned the client reports to provide a clearer picture of year-over-year progress
Accounts Consultant	1988–91	Preparing client monthly reports on sales and promotions activities	

Training Undertaken	Instructor/ Organization	Date	Description	What I Learned
Effective management	Lars Toeplast Peak Managers Blue Mountains	1991	Wilderness course on teamwork and delegation	Taught me to set clear goals and listen to others in a group

On Worksheet 2 list the following:
- All the jobs you held
- The names of the companies
- The titles of your jobs
- Your responsibilities
- Your reason for leaving
- Your achievements (which we will discuss in more detail in Chapter 7)
- Any promotions.

Worksheet 3: Life

Activity	Dates	Description	Achievements/ Personal Development	Possible Relevance to Job

Worksheet 3: Life (Example)

Activity	Dates	Description	Achievements/ Personal Development	Possible Relevance to Job
Community work	1990 to date	Bookkeeping for local branch of St. Vincent de Paul	Satisfaction of giving something back to local community	Shows energy to use my accounting skills outside of normal areas
Hobbies interests	1992 to date	Breeding pedigree Welsh Springer Spaniels	Won best of breed, best overall at Country Show	To be a breeder requires responsibility/ commitment and maturity
Sports	1979 to date	Basketball, at school, and now for the Springfield Tigers	Social life, helps keep me fit	Helps me be a team player Reduces stress

Activity	Dates	Description	Achievements/ Personal Development	Possible Relevance to Job
Other	1994	On the organizing committee of the Festival of Food, a two-week festival aimed at promoting the local restaurants and raising awareness about diet		Good organizational skills

On Worksheet 3, include any extracurricular activities:

- Sports
- Committees
- Interest groups (for example, amateur drama)
- Training courses (such as wine appreciation, motor mechanics, and so on)
- Charitable work
- Hobbies

➤ **Tip:** Do a lot with your life so that there is good, interesting material to include in a well presented resume! This may seem a little harsh (and obvious), but remember that this is from the horse's (the employers') mouth!

Employers talk a lot about their employees "making a contribution," so if you can demonstrate this in your resume, you will be a more attractive candidate. The more time you spend away from passive activities such as watching television, the more likely it is that you will have positive things to say on your resume. Think for one minute how society views people who do nothing but watch television in their leisure time. They are called "couch potatoes," or worse, and this is especially damning for younger people.

List Your Achievements for Each Part of Your Life

It is surprising how quickly some people can forget what they have achieved or play down their role in successes. Sometimes this is because you are not feeling too good about yourself. You may have lost your job, or been unemployed or out of the workforce for a long time. You must learn to recognize the symptoms if you are playing down your achievements. It is amazing, but we have seen countless university students who hold excellent undergraduate degrees and Masters or Ph.D. degrees who say "But I haven't really achieved anything."

Look closely at all the activities you have listed in each period of your life. Now think really carefully about anything that you might have achieved during this time. It might be useful for you to dip into Chapter 8 now and have a look at our "Gestalt Rule of Proximity." It states that people will credit you with an achievement if you were sufficiently close to it. For example, if you were a member of a team that saw sales increase by 20 percent annually, you should claim it as an achievement, even if you can't say for sure exactly how much of that outcome was directly related to your efforts.

Achievements and Facts: A Balancing Act

If you look at our worksheets, you will see that they are divided roughly down the middle. On the left side are the dates and jobs and hobbies. On the right side, we have the achievements, the promotions, and the personal development.

Names, dates & numbers   Achievements

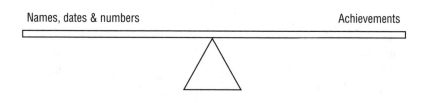
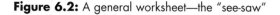

Figure 6.2: A general worksheet—the "see-saw"

It is our experience that people are great at loading the left side of the see-saw while they tend to forget the right side. Why is this? Some reasons why people focus on "names, dates, and numbers" include the following:

- They are easier to remember
- People are taught to be modest
- Names, dates, and numbers are easier to confirm
- Some people get lazy, letting the names and dates speak for them
- Writing them out doesn't take much thinking

We believe very strongly that achievements are extremely important. You can see from Figure 6.2 that excluding achievements will lead to an unbalanced resume.

This leads us to the next two golden rules:

> Resumes exist to tell the world what you have achieved.
>
> Achievements count. Everybody has achievements; some are just better at hiding them than others.

Here are some examples to help you. Check our list of possible achievements:
- Earning promotions
- Increasing sales figures
- Running a project to change something in your company
- Being part of a team that… (what did your team do?)
- Winning an award or prize (no matter how trivial, list it)
- Achieving good results in exams or assessments
- Gaining qualifications (such as a degree or a chauffeur's license)
- Winning the employee of the month award
- Winning customer service/quality awards
- Participating in outside-work achievements, such as raising money for charity or being elected to a committee
- Winning a league or a race; captaining a sports team
- Going long periods without absence from work (such as no sick days in three years)
- Running a marathon or a fun run
- Helping to paint a school/community center
- Implementing or designing systems or processes
- Improving efficiencies or overhauling processes

At the end of this chapter, you should have three completed worksheets, and they should look well balanced. That is, the right and left sides should both have plenty of information.

Well done! You now have most of the ingredients you require to build a great resume. Before we do that, in the next chapter we will consider the final ingredient—you!

Keeping a resume up-to-date is essential because you never know when you might need to apply for a new job. Jim Bright and Robert Pryor have developed a Chaos Theory of Career Development. Part of the theory is that people choose jobs on the basis of chance or unplanned events. They found that 70 percent of a large sample of people said their careers had been influenced significantly by a chance event. Lucy Harpham and Jim Bright followed this up and replicated the finding—the majority of people will have their careers influenced by a chance event. So you never know when you'll need your resume in a hurry!

CHAPTER 7

What Sort of Person Are You?

In this chapter, you will learn
- What qualities employers look for
- what these qualities mean in practice
- How to check whether you possess these qualities

Let's face it, work takes up a major part of our time, so it stands to reason that people want to work with colleagues who are pleasant and easy to get along with. If you had to choose between two equally talented co-workers—one you hated, and one you liked—would there really be any decision to make? Increasingly, companies are becoming aware that their employees' personal habits and their work personality not only influence the harmony of the workforce, but may directly influence the quality of the work done, too.

Many job ads these days list the personal qualities companies believe are important to be successful in their organizations. Many companies take this information very seriously and some will use quite sophisticated psychological tests to measure your ability to work in a team, or how quickly you might lose your temper. Other companies will invite you to join a group of other applicants to assess how well you interact with others.

Generally this sort of information is collected after reading your resume—in interviews and so on—but it is a good idea to emphasize on your resume that you will fit the company's desired "personality." In this chapter, we highlight some of the most common "psychological" traits that employers look for, explain what they mean, and demonstrate how to emphasize your strengths in these areas.

What Are the Most Common Qualities Employers Look For?

From a consideration of job advertisements, the following is our list of the eight most popular qualities desired by employers:

- Communication skills, verbal and written
- Team skills/team player
- Attention to detail
- Energy/dynamism/achievement/drive
- Initiative
- Ability to handle pressure
- Enthusiasm
- Leadership

What Do Employers Want When They Ask for These Qualities?

Let's consider these skills in order.

Communication Skills

This is so common that you should assume that every job requires them—and employers say so too! Assume that communication skills are important for every job and try to demonstrate them in your resume. There is a mountain of evidence from research on employment interviews that candidates demonstrating good communication skills tend to get the highest ratings. There is no reason why you can't demonstrate these skills in your resume.

Who Will You Communicate With?

The type and degree of skill you need to demonstrate will depend on the type of job you are going for. The job might involve communicating with any of the following:

- People in your team or department
- Other departments in the same organization
- Other organizations, or with the public
- Special groups, such as the young or elderly
- Influential or senior clients such as corporate sponsors
- Lawyers
- Government officials
- Senior managers

What difference does it make who you communicate with? Different situations make different demands on you and you should be aware of the sort of communication you may need. While an employer might tolerate the occasional gruff tone or mildly sarcastic remark within the confines of the office, a very dim view will be taken of such behavior in front of clients.

Look at the job ad or description and try to establish who you might be communicating with the most. The skills required may range from being able to understand and relay telephone messages clearly to writing an extensive report or proposal, or presenting a sales pitch to customers.

Questions to ask yourself are the following:

- Do I speak clearly in English?
- Can I write clearly?
- Am I able to understand what people are saying to me on most occasions?
- Can I explain things to people clearly?

So How Do I Demonstrate These Skills on My Resume?

You could draw on your work history. For instance, passing a typing test might suggest you can spell accurately, as would shorthand skills. Work as a receptionist or a sales representative suggests that you can communicate verbally and effectively. Giving presentations to clients, or other public speaking experience such as Toastmasters, looks good.

Team Skills

What this means is that you are happy and effective working in groups with other people. You are happy to work together, share information, and help out team members when they are struggling. You tend to like people, and are reasonably well liked. It sometimes seems that "team player" is added to just about every job ad without any real reason. As a general rule, it is code for saying "Do you get along with other people, or are you selfish and unpleasant?" Some people think the expression "team player" refers to membership in sporting teams. Generally, this is not the case, and it is better to use examples of your team skills drawn from work experience. Of course, if you cannot think of any convincing examples from work, then you might consider using some limited examples from your hobbies.

Attention to Detail

Many jobs request this skill. Just because this quality is not included in an advertisement, do not assume it is not important. Making silly mistakes in some jobs, such as an accounting clerk position where large sums of money may be involved, can lead to very expensive outcomes! In a study we conducted, where we deliberately included spelling mistakes on some resumes but not on others, we found that even one error reduced the chance of the candidate being interviewed by between 30 and 45 percent. Think about it—just a minor error can reduce your chances of being interviewed by almost half!

Spelling errors and typos, bad grammar, and poor phrasing were some of the problems with resumes most frequently mentioned by the recruiters we interviewed. Make sure there are no spelling mistakes. Use the spellchecker. Ensure your grammar and punctuation are correct. If you are going to claim that you have good attention to detail, then demonstrate it on your resume by making sure it is completely free of mistakes.

One recent example of a resume we saw from a student read: "I have excellent attention to deatail"! Not only does this sentence undermine itself, it sends out warning signals—what other weaknesses does this candidate have?

Energy, Dynamism, Enthusiasm, Drive, and Initiative

Nobody wants to employ somebody who slumps in their seat, seems to take forever to carry out the most trivial tasks, and sighs deeply every time they are asked to do something. The organization looking for these qualities is looking for someone who is alert, gets on with their work quickly and without unnecessary complaint, and (within reason) will find solutions to problems rather than find problems with solutions.

You are only human, so it is okay to feel lousy from time to time—there is nothing more irritating or downright suspect than the person who is always ecstatically happy. Do remember, though, that your resume is not the place for a display of negativity.

Ability to Handle Pressure

Pressure varies from job to job, but the request for this ability is an indication that things might get very busy from time to time—for example, work in a fire department or with the police force, where lapses of concentration or failures of nerve have potentially fatal outcomes. What the employer wants to see is evidence that you will respond to the challenge and perhaps work faster or longer hours on occasion to meet deadlines or reduce the backlog. What they are saying is they do not expect you to lose your temper or take sick leave at the first sign of pressure. Pressure in some jobs will be immediate, such as a long line of irritated customers. Or it could be longer-term stress, such as the pressure to build all the stadiums for the Olympic Games on time!

Leadership

Leadership is one of those qualities that tends to get thrown into a job ad without much justification. For a start, nobody can agree on what makes a good leader.

However, if you can demonstrate that you have managed a team of people success-fully—either by length of time in the position (this says that if you were not a good leader you would have been moved on quickly), or by tasks achieved by a group under your management—this may be the sort of thing the employer is looking for. Equally, being elected to a chairperson's role or similar job would sug-gest that you inspire the confidence of others.

Be careful not to confuse strong-mindedness with leadership. The person who charges off from the social group in one direction, only to see the rest of the group subsequently set off in another direction, is demonstrating their hot-headedness, not leadership.

How Do You Rate Against the List of Important Skills?

Here are a few questions that might help you think about these skills in relation to yourself. Use these questions to trigger ideas about your own personal qualities.

- Do you tend to get details right more often than not, or do you find details irritating?
- Do you prefer working in a team of people, or on your own?
- Do you like to be a leader, or a team member?
- Are you punctual for work?
- Would you say you are outgoing and like meeting people and going to par-ties, or do you prefer your own company or just a few trusted friends?
- Do you tend to be cheerful and positive, or do you get easily depressed?
- When people make a lot of demands on you, do you tend to remain calm, or do you find yourself losing your temper?

All of the above questions are commonly asked of candidates by employers because they are regarded as important qualities in successful employees. You may be thinking that to any or all of those questions your answer is "Sometimes yes, sometimes no," or "It depends," or "It is not as simple as that." That is a perfect-ly reasonable response. The point is, if these are the qualities sought by employers, the more you can demonstrate them through deeds, the better.

Exercising Your Skills

The following exercises should help you address the "personality requirements" of employers more easily.

Communication Skills Exercise

The following worksheet will help you identify and write your communication skills.

Communication Skills Worksheet

List the people or group of people that you commonly communicate with. Next to each person or group of people, write down how you communicate. Is it face to face, in writing, or on the phone? What is your presentation style? Then write down how you know what you're communicating has been successful. Take a look at our example, then add your own list.

Who	Communication Method	Evidence of Success
Managing director	Face-to-face questions	Body language, no clarification needed
Unit leader	Presentation of monthly reports	Identified by board as able to coach others

Teamwork and Leadership Exercises

Many companies will be fairly clear whether they want a leader or a team member (or both). Looking like a leader when a team member is called for will have recruiters thinking that you will not take direction and will question decisions. Equally, if a leader is required, looking too much like "one of the boys" might be interpreted as being a poor leader.

Writing Co-Worker Relations Statements

List examples of your ability to get along well with co-workers. Here are a few examples to guide you:

- "The restructure motivated my new team, and we all took on extra duties to ensure that we accomplished our goals, which we actually exceeded every month."
- "Five of us were assigned to investigate why our customer service ratings were down. We divided the tasks up into different product areas and decided on weekly team meetings. We soon discovered that there were some common problems, and our recommendations when implemented, proved very popular."
- "I took on a departed colleague's duties to ensure a smooth transition before a replacement was recruited for our team."
- "I was voted most popular employee twice last year."
- _____
- _____
- _____
- _____
- _____

Writing Team Membership Statements

Try writing your own statements to show you are outgoing, like meeting people, going to parties, or that you prefer your own company, or just a few trusted friends. Our examples follow:

- "I enjoy public speaking."
- "I am the staff social representative."
- "I enjoy dealing with my customers."
- "I enjoyed my five years in sales."
- _____
- _____
- _____
- _____
- _____

Avoid Appearing Antisocial

There are few jobs that would openly seek people who are not outgoing, but they do exist. Any job where contact with other employees or the public is not frequent would be a case in point. Such jobs include machine operators, back-room processing jobs, or jobs where people are out "on the road" alone, like truck drivers or people working from home. Inadvertent statements that may make you look a little antisocial would be

- *"I have learned to be very self-reliant."*
- *"I worked in sole practice for 20 years."*
- *"I enjoy the challenge of myself-against-the-elements on wilderness retreats."*

Writing Leadership Statements

The following are some sample statements showing leadership:

- "I reorganized the way payments were processed. This involved reassigning several staff, some job enlargement, and the layoff of three staff members."
- "Under my management, the group has shown record profits in the past eight quarters."
- _____
- _____
- _____

Attention to Detail Exercise

The following worksheet will help you quantify examples of your attention to detail.

Detail Worksheet

List work tasks or, preferably, results where your attention to detail has been demonstrated. For example:

- "I have never had documents I have typed sent back to me with factual or grammatical errors in them."
- "During my time in this post, I reduced the amount of internal mail that was incorrectly addressed by more than 30 percent."
- _____
- _____
- _____
- _____
- _____

Energy, Enthusiasm, and Initiative Exercise

This exercise will help you demonstrate your energy, enthusiasm, and initiative.

Energy, Enthusiasm, and Initiative Worksheet

Try writing your own statements after reading these samples:

- "My project required me to identify better ways of doing things in the accounting department to increase productivity and customer satisfaction. Mustering the talent of our finance department, I solicited employee ideas and persuaded management to award the best idea a $500 incentive. These ideas resulted in savings of over $500,000 to the company."
- "I was given the task of reorganizing client files to better improve storage and retrieval. Although this was an area in which I had limited experience, I contacted my colleagues in other parts of the company and, by sharing ideas with them and working long hours, I implemented a new system within two weeks (three weeks earlier than my manager expected)."

- _____
- _____
- _____
- _____
- _____

Pressure Exercises

Statements that show your calm temperament, or ability to handle pressure, might look like this:

- "My current role regularly involves having to produce briefing reports on extremely short notice. It is satisfying to get the job done against apparently impossible odds."
- "A key skill is my ability to calm down angry passengers whose flights have been delayed."

If there was a time when a job had to be finished by a deadline and you worked overnight or over the weekend to complete it, write down the details next to the relevant job.

Pressure Worksheet

Job	Details of Pressure Situation

Finally, reflect on the places where you have worked, the times you have worked (such as nightshifts or overtime), and the bosses you have worked for. Are there any things that stand out as particularly good or bad?

Where Wouldn't You Work?

Now is the time to make a list of things you will not put up with in the workplace. To do this, make three lists with the following headings:

1. I will never work in a place that....
2. I will only put up with...if it happens very rarely.
3. I would prefer not to work in a place that...but I know I can cope if necessary.

The things you might put on one of these lists include

- Bad-tempered boss
- Lots of people smoking
- Few people of my gender or ethnic background at work
- Premises in the middle of town
- Premises out of town
- No free or convenient parking
- Very poor safety record

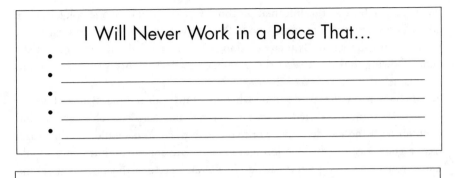

I Will Never Work in a Place That...

- _____
- _____
- _____
- _____
- _____

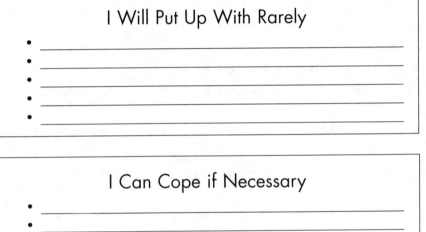

I Will Put Up With Rarely

- _____
- _____
- _____
- _____
- _____

I Can Cope if Necessary

- _____
- _____
- _____
- _____
- _____

Your Pantry of Ingredients

You should now have several worksheets listing all the things that you have done over your working life, and how you see yourself. Think of this as your "pantry" of ingredients. This is what we will use to make your tailored resume, and it brings us to our next golden rule.

Take time every couple of months to update your skills and achievements list. This way you will always have an up-to-date list and you are less likely to forget your achievements over time.

Now that you have all this information about yourself, you have one task left. Give all the information to somebody who knows you very well, and who you trust. Ask them "Is this me?" and "Is there anything I've left out?" If you are embarrassed about showing someone else all those immodest achievements we've asked you to list, blame us! We told you to do it.

You are now ready to start deciding what goes into your resume. Before choosing a style of resume, you need to start matching your personal achievements and qualities with the job detective work you have done. You should, by this stage, have a good idea of what the job requirements are and this information should guide you in choosing which achievements and personal qualities you should include. The challenge here varies for different groups. Use our Work History Achievement Chart (Table 7.1) to assist you in this task.

Table 7.1: Work History Achievement Chart

Career Stage	Information to Emphasize	Key Challenges for Your Resume
High school graduate	Educational qualifications; personality/life skills; community involvement; any work experience; your age (so people do not expect too much work experience if you are young); hobbies	Demonstrate to an employer what you have some skills to offer (either through your education or through community involvement. Demonstrate readiness to enter the workforce through responsibility, reliability, and maturity.
College graduate	Qualifications; any work experience, including informational visits and internships as a part of your studies; awards; community involvement; personality/life skills	Show an employer that you are more than just a brain, that you are well rounded, are involved in things outside study, and you have not wasted the opportunities that college offers. Demonstrate evidence of responsibility, leadership, maturity and, if relevant, commercial awareness.

continued

continued

Career Stage	Information to Emphasize	Key Challenges for Your Resume
Early career	Qualifications; work experience; work achievements; personality; life skills	Show how you have progressed and what new skills you've learned in the workforce. Show a logical pattern in your work history that tells a story, and that this job is the logical next step.
Mid-career	Work experience, especially the past five years and anything relevant to the position applied for; work achievements; Positions of leadership/responsibility; relevant training courses or industry qualifications; membership in professional associations	Demonstrate a period of sustained success and recognition at work. The story needs to tell of a steady (or faster) rise up the organizational ladder, or alternatively, a steady (or better) stream of achievement and recognition. Show a broadening of your industry experience or mastery of your chosen skill.
Late career	Leadership and management skills or mastery of a set of skills; wide experience across situations, organizations, and/or countries; professional recognition of your status	Show that you can fit into the organization and help out from day one. Demonstrate a track record of success. Come across as totally sound and remove any doubts that you can do the job with assurance.

continued

continued

Career Stage	Information to Emphasize	Key Challenges for Your Resume
Career change	Transferable skills, any skills or experience that may be relevant to the chosen career; any skills acquired in a previous career relevant to the one you are choosing; evidence of personal qualities such as flexibility and willingness to learn	Think about your current work experience from an outsider's perspective. Can you portray mundane skills in a new light that makes them seem relevant? Convince the recruiter that this is a considered move and a logical progression or sensible change. Minimize the differences between you and the new job.
Re-entry into the workforce after a break	Qualifications that are still current; any activities and achievements in the time away from work; efforts to keep yourself up to date with current market knowledge; personal qualities that are relevant to the job and that show market/ commercial awareness	Show that you are not completely out of touch and that you have something very valuable to offer that ideally will not cost the company a lot of time and money to develop. Demonstrate that you spent your time out of the workforce responsibly and productively. Be aware that your reasons for being out of the workforce may not be highly valued by the employer.

CHAPTER 8

Making the Perfect Fit

In this chapter, you will learn
- *What chronological, functional, hybrid, and structured interview resumes look like*
- *How to tailor a resume for you and the job*

How Do I Set Up My Resume?

There are several different ways of writing a resume. Different approaches work for different people. The three most popular resume styles are these:

- Chronological resumes
- Functional resumes
- Hybrid resumes

To these three we will also add the structured interview resume. Although not used often, this resume format enables a person to set out the benefits that they offer an employer in a conversational style. It is inviting to read and enables you to convey a lot of targeted information. It is particularly useful if you are able to anticipate the types of questions that will be asked at an interview. By presenting your resume in this way, you provide the employer with an expectation about how you might perform in an interview, giving the employer a reason to consider your application further.

The Chronological Resume

This resume style is the one many people use without thinking. It lists your training and jobs in order of the dates you started each of them. Typically, people list their most recent training or jobs first and proceed backwards to the first things they did in the past. This is called "reverse chronological" order.

The components of this resume are these:

1. Personal contact information
2. Employment history, including the following:
   - Employers
   - Dates of employment
   - Positions held
   - Achievements

3. Educational qualifications
4. Professional development/training courses

Here is an example of a chronological resume.

Robert Brown

10 Elm Ave.   bbrown@aol.com   (H) (312) 111-3111
Springville, IL 60606   (W) (312) 111-2111

Employment History

Jones Bros., Inc.   **3/2003 to Present**
*Jones Bros. is a large national company that owns a range of goods transportation systems. Next-Day Freight provides
distribution systems for a broad customer base, including a range of major companies.*

State Manager for Next-Day Freight, Chicago, IL

Reporting to the General Manager, major responsibilities in this position include acting as a
change agent reshaping the business into a professional and profitable organization with a strong
emphasis on customer service. The bottom-line responsibility of this position is a $50 million
business unit employing 350 people in sales, administration, operations, marketing, customer
service, quality, and security.

Major Achievements:
- Created and implemented a state business plan addressing major shortfalls
  in the business.
- Orchestrated a successful merger with another $10 million business unit.
- Restructured the entire sales force.
- Negotiated and implemented a new enterprise agreement.
- Directed a complete management restructure.
- Introduced new Management Information Systems.
- Negotiated the outsourcing of $2.5 million in annual casual labor.
- Coordinated the rebuilding of a major new depot facility.
- Implemented a quantifiable quality improvement program.
- Developed a new marketing strategy.
- Developed a major strategic industrial relations plan to create greater incentives
  for the workforce.
- Led the business unit to its best profit performance.

National Petroleum, Inc.   **2/1991 to 2/2003**
*National is a major petroleum company that owns refineries throughout North America,
as well as a major franchise network of automotive fuel stations.*

National Distribution Network Manager, Des Moines, IA   *3/1998 to 2/2003*

Reporting to the National Planning Manager, responsible for the strategic development and
network rationalization of the wholesale distribution business worth more than $80 million per
year to company profit. Maintained primary trade and developed an environment for improved
profit performance based on best practices, operating efficiency, and optimum capital investment.

Major Achievements:
- Performed comprehensive review of the sector and developed an integrated business
  plan for the next century.
- Developed a new network process to contain the best demographic mix of distribution
  and marketing.
- Developed and implemented a merchandising-based franchise package.
- Implemented a business planning process for independent distributors.
- Directed the strategic business review of a $300 million subsidiary.
- Managed the wholesale investment budget to achieve corporate objectives.
- Successfully rationalized and restructured the distributor business to improve the
  return on investment.

(continued)

Figure 8.1: A chronological resume.

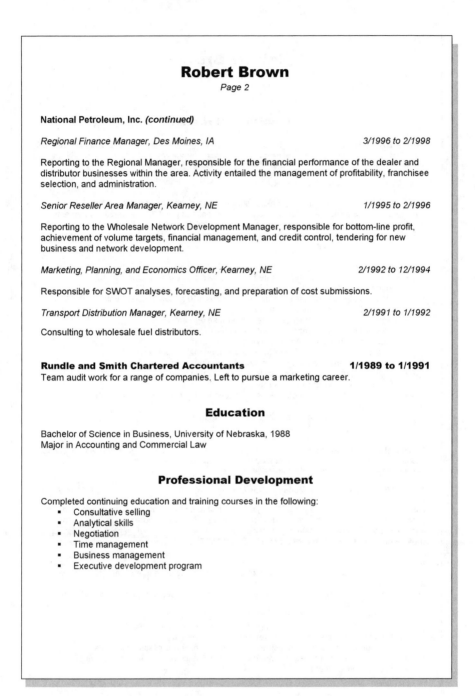

Robert Brown
Page 2

National Petroleum, Inc. *(continued)*

Regional Finance Manager, Des Moines, IA   *3/1996 to 2/1998*

Reporting to the Regional Manager, responsible for the financial performance of the dealer and distributor businesses within the area. Activity entailed the management of profitability, franchisee selection, and administration.

Senior Reseller Area Manager, Kearney, NE   *1/1995 to 2/1996*

Reporting to the Wholesale Network Development Manager, responsible for bottom-line profit, achievement of volume targets, financial management, and credit control, tendering for new business and network development.

Marketing, Planning, and Economics Officer, Kearney, NE   *2/1992 to 12/1994*

Responsible for SWOT analyses, forecasting, and preparation of cost submissions.

Transport Distribution Manager, Kearney, NE   *2/1991 to 1/1992*

Consulting to wholesale fuel distributors.

Rundle and Smith Chartered Accountants   **1/1989 to 1/1991**
Team audit work for a range of companies. Left to pursue a marketing career.

Education

Bachelor of Science in Business, University of Nebraska, 1988
Major in Accounting and Commercial Law

Professional Development

Completed continuing education and training courses in the following:
- Consultative selling
- Analytical skills
- Negotiation
- Time management
- Business management
- Executive development program

The Functional Resume

This is a style that emphasizes the skills of the individual and his or her achievements. It is often used when the applicant lacks formal education, or their educational qualifications are judged obsolete or irrelevant. If you have had many different jobs with no clear pattern of progression, or a lot of gaps in your work history, some people recommend this approach. You do not, after all, want to present your career as a drunken stagger through the world of work!

Figure 8.2 is an example of a functional resume.

Robert Brown

10 Elm Ave.   bbrown@aol.com   (H) (312) 111-3111
Springville, IL 60606   (W) (312) 111-2111

Skills, Knowledge, Attributes, and Abilities

Communication Skills
In role as State Manager for Next-Day Freight, required to liaise across a broad cross-section of employees. To keep employees abreast of company direction and anticipated changes, implemented briefing sessions to be held across all shifts once a month. Communicated directly with the staff and fielded questions. Employee satisfaction regarding communications improved from 2.5 to 4.3 over a 12-month period.

Business Management
Sound knowledge of business management principles. Studied commerce at NU and keep current with recent trends and developments by subscribing to journals and magazines. Training courses include the AGSM Executive Development Program and specialist management courses. Over the past three years, have implemented ideas gained from knowledge to restructure the sales force and supervise the implementation of a new management information system and quality improvement program.

Selling Skills
As National Distribution Network Manager for National Petroleum, Inc., developed a merchandising-based franchise package aimed at convincing successful franchisees with other companies to join National Petroleum. Developed a program that targeted the top 100 successful franchisees and, by interviewing a cross-section, identified reasons why most would convert. Developed a selling kit for representatives to use and conducted selling skills training courses for representatives. Worked with the top three clients personally and all three converted. Of the remaining 97 franchisees, 70 percent converted.

Negotiation Skills
As State Manager for Next-Day Freight, address numerous issues regarding workforce planning. This includes outsourcing $2.5 million worth of casual labor, implementing a staff incentive program, and developing a new enterprise agreement. These represented major changes for our existing and often volatile workforce. By developing and chairing a committee involving employee, management, and union representatives, we have been able to successfully introduce the required changes without any lost time. Employee satisfaction with working conditions has risen from 1.8 to 4.0 over the past three years.

Tenacity
On promotion to the position of State Manager for Next-Day Freight, quickly identified potential cost savings in merging our business unit with our sister company's (Parcel Pick-Up) business unit worth $10 million. The project to merge the two units was realized last month after planning and negotiations spanning more than three years. Anticipated cost savings as a result of the merger are likely to be in the vicinity of $5 billion.

Summary of Employment History

3/03 to Present	Jones Bros., Inc., State Manager—Next-Day Freight
3/98 to 2/03	National Petroleum, Inc., National Distribution Network Manager
3/96 to 2/98	National Petroleum, Inc., Regional Finance Manager
1/95 to 2/96	National Petroleum, Inc., Senior Reseller Area Manager
2/92 to 12/94	National Petroleum, Inc., Marketing, Planning, and Economics Officer
2/91 to 1/92	National Petroleum, Inc., Transport Distribution Manager
1/89 to 1/91	Rundle and Smith, Team Auditor

Education

Bachelor of Science in Business, University of Nebraska, 1988
Major in Accounting and Commercial Law

Figure 8.2: A functional resume.

The Hybrid Resume

This is an increasingly popular approach that combines the best of both the chronological resume and the functional resume. A hybrid resume retains much of the fixed order of the chronological resume, but there is a lot more emphasis on skills and achievements—sometimes in a separate section.

The hybrid approach is the one that we recommend to most people, in that it produces an excellent clear structure but requires the candidate to really think hard about their achievements and what they have to offer. Obviously, there is a limit to how long your resume should be. If you decide to use a hybrid style, you may wish to leave out the detailed responsibilities section and just emphasize the skills, knowledge, and abilities you have.

Figure 8.3 is an example of a hybrid resume.

Robert Brown

10 Elm Ave.   bbrown@aol.com   (H) (312) 111-3111
Springville, IL 60606   (W) (312) 111-2111

Skills, Knowledge, Attributes, and Abilities

Communication Skills
In role as State Manager for Next-Day Freight, required to liaise across a broad cross-section of employees. To keep employees abreast of company direction and anticipated changes, implemented briefing sessions to be held across all shifts once a month. Communicated directly with the staff and fielded questions. Employee satisfaction regarding communications improved from 2.5 to 4.3 over a 12-month period.

Business Management
Sound knowledge of business management principles. Studied commerce at NU and keep current with recent trends and developments by subscribing to journals and magazines. Training courses include the AGSM Executive Development Program and specialist management courses. Over the past three years, have implemented ideas gained from knowledge to restructure the sales force and supervise the implementation of a new management information system and quality improvement program.

Selling Skills
As National Distribution Network Manager for National Petroleum, Inc., developed a merchandising-based franchise package aimed at convincing successful franchisees with other companies to join National Petroleum. Developed a program that targeted the top 100 successful franchisees and, by interviewing a cross-section, identified reasons why most would convert. Developed a selling kit for representatives to use and conducted selling skills training courses for representatives. Worked with the top three clients personally and all three converted. Of the remaining 97 franchisees, 70 percent converted.

Negotiation Skills
As State Manager for Next-Day Freight, address numerous issues regarding workforce planning. This includes outsourcing $2.5 million worth of casual labor, implementing a staff incentive program, and developing a new enterprise agreement. These represented major changes for our existing and often volatile workforce. By developing and chairing a committee involving employee, management, and union representatives, we have been able to successfully introduce the required changes without any lost time. Employee satisfaction with working conditions has risen from 1.8 to 4.0 over the past three years.

Tenacity
On promotion to the position of State Manager for Next-Day Freight, quickly identified potential cost savings in merging our business unit with our sister company's (Parcel Pick-Up) business unit worth $10 million. The project to merge the two units was realized last month after planning and negotiations spanning more than three years. Anticipated cost savings as a result of the merger are likely to be in the vicinity of $5 billion.

Employment History

Jones Bros., Inc.   **3/2003 to Present**
Jones Bros. is a large national company that owns a range of goods transportation systems. Next-Day Freight provides distribution systems for a broad customer base, including a range of major companies.

State Manager for Next-Day Freight, Chicago, IL

Reporting to the General Manager, major responsibilities in this position include acting as a change agent reshaping the business into a professional and profitable organization with a strong emphasis on customer service. The bottom-line responsibility of this position is a $50 million business unit employing 350 people in sales, administration, operations, marketing, customer service, quality, and security.

Major Achievements:
- Created and implemented a state business plan addressing major shortfalls in the business.
- Orchestrated a successful merger with another $10 million business unit.
- Restructured the entire sales force.
- Negotiated and implemented a new enterprise agreement.
- Directed a complete management restructure.
- Introduced new Management Information Systems.
- Negotiated the outsourcing of $2.5 million in annual casual labor.

Figure 8.3: A hybrid resume.

Robert Brown
Page 2

Jones Bros., Inc. *(continued)*

- Coordinated the rebuilding of a major new depot facility.
- Implemented a quantifiable quality improvement program.
- Developed a new marketing strategy.
- Developed strategic industrial relations plan to create greater incentives for the workforce.
- Led the business unit to its best profit performance.

National Petroleum, Inc.   **2/1991 to 2/2003**
*National is a major petroleum company that owns refineries throughout North America,
as well as a major franchise network of automotive fuel stations.*

National Distribution Network Manager, Des Moines, IA   *3/1998 to 2/2003*

Reporting to the National Planning Manager, responsible for the strategic development and network rationalization of the wholesale distribution business worth more than $80 million per year to company profit. Maintained primary trade and developed an environment for improved profit performance based on best practices, operating efficiency, and optimum capital investment.

Major Achievements:
- Performed comprehensive review of the sector and developed an integrated business plan.
- Developed a new network process to contain the best demographic mix of distribution and marketing.
- Developed and implemented a merchandising-based franchise package.
- Implemented a business planning process for independent distributors.
- Directed the strategic business review of a $300 million subsidiary.
- Managed the wholesale investment budget to achieve corporate objectives.
- Successfully rationalized and restructured the distributor business to improve return on investment.

Regional Finance Manager, Des Moines, IA   *3/1996 to 2/1998*

Reporting to the Regional Manager, responsible for the financial performance of the dealer and distributor businesses within the area. Activity entailed the management of profitability, franchisee selection, and administration.

Senior Reseller Area Manager, Kearney, NE   *1/1995 to 2/1996*

Reporting to the Wholesale Network Development Manager, responsible for bottom-line profit, achievement of volume targets, financial management, and credit control, tendering for new business and network development.

Marketing, Planning, and Economics Officer, Kearney, NE   *2/1992 to 12/1994*

Responsible for SWOT analyses, forecasting, and preparation of cost submissions.

Transport Distribution Manager, Kearney, NE   *2/1991 to 1/1992*

Consulting to wholesale fuel distributors.

Rundle and Smith Chartered Accountants   **1/1989 to 1/1991**
Team audit work for a range of companies. Left to pursue a marketing career.

Education

Bachelor of Science in Business, University of Nebraska, 1988
Major in Accounting and Commercial Law

Professional Development

Completed continuing education and training courses in consultative selling, analytical skills, negotiation, time management, business management, and executive development.

The Structured Interview Resume

This is an idea that might work for some people. In a structured interview, the job applicant is asked a series of questions in a set order. In a structured interview resume, the candidate sets out a series of questions and provides the answers to them. Increasingly, these types of questions are being asked on Web-based job application forms, so setting up your resume in this manner may elicit a positive response from the employer. This approach emphasizes skills and competencies over formal qualifications. The following questions are examples of the types of questions that can be used to make up a structured interview resume.

Communication Skills
- What types of proposals have you written?
- What are some of the most difficult groups you've had to present to?

Business Management
- How does your experience in business management match our job requirements?

Selling Skills
- What has been the toughest selling assignment you have ever had?

Negotiation Skills
- What do you believe are the successful outcomes of a good negotiation process?
- When have you demonstrated your negotiation skills?

Tenacity
- Describe a project or work assignment that best demonstrates your tenacity.

Structured Interview Resume Example
Let's look at our sample resume, presented as a structured interview (Figure 8.4).

Robert Brown

10 Elm Ave.   bbrown@aol.com   (H) (312) 111-3111
Springville, IL 60606   (W) (312) 111-2111

Employers

2003 to Present, Jones Bros., Inc. (Next-Day Freight)
1991–2003, National Petroleum, Inc.

Education

Bachelor of Science in Business, University of Nebraska, 1988
Major in Accounting and Commercial Law

Professional Development

Completed continuing education and training courses in the following:
- Consultative selling
- Analytical skills
- Negotiation
- Time management
- Business management
- Executive development program

Skills, Knowledge, Attributes, and Abilities

Communication Skills

What types of proposals have you written?
I have written a wide range of proposals, in terms of significance and audience. Proposals have included change in marketing strategy proposals for presentation to board of directors; industrial relations proposals for presentation to board of directors and union organizers; a prospectus for potential franchisees; merger recommendations for presentation to our board of directors and to the board of directors of the proposed merging company.

What are some of the most difficult groups you've had to present to?
Although I have had no "difficult groups" as such, I have needed to present to some quite skeptical and cautious groups. These have included union organizers, potential franchisees, and the board of directors of a company we were proposing to merge with. All groups were significant stakeholders with a lot to lose from a poor decision; and consequently, there were a lot of questions to field and I was forced to think quickly. Presentations were designed to address the audiences' primary concerns in a style that they were most comfortable with. In the preceding examples, my presentations contributed to successful outcomes in all three cases.

Business Management

How does your experience in business management match our job requirements?
Over the past nine years, my jobs have primarily focused on business management. I have a broad background in most aspects of general management, including finance, sales, marketing, distribution, business development, and, most recently, human resources, in my role as state manager. My experience is complemented by formal studies in accounting and commercial law, demonstrating that I can successfully convert theory into practice. I have the necessary breadth and depth of experience to fulfill or exceed requirements as the national manager for Overnight-Now.

Selling Skills

What has been the toughest selling assignment you have ever had?
The toughest selling assignment has been convincing existing successful franchisees to change to National Petroleum. Already proven to be successful with GDP Petrol, these franchisees had more to gain by converting to National Petroleum, but naturally some were skeptical. I went about finding the franchisees' most frequent

Figure 8.4: A structured interview resume.

source of dissatisfaction with GDP and structured a package that addressed these concerns. Because there were 100 franchisees to convert, I could not handle all of these myself. By training our representatives, 97 franchisees were approached, of which 70 percent converted. I managed the relationship with the top three franchisees personally, and all converted.

Negotiation Skills

What do you believe are the successful outcomes of a good negotiation process?
A genuine win-win result for both parties. I think it is important to go into a negotiation with a clear understanding of what I want to achieve, as well as being prepared to listen to what the other party wants. At the end of the negotiation there needs to be a set of outcomes agreed to and honored by both parties.

When have you best demonstrated your negotiation skills?
During our enterprise agreement negotiation at Next-Day Freight. Management wanted to introduce significant changes to the types of skills, shift rosters, and duties performed by employees to deliver maximum workforce flexibility in our 1998 negotiations. These changes represented significant cost savings to the business as well as ensuring longer-term business viability. Without these changes, it was likely that the business would need to retrench many of its current permanent workforce and outsource functions to contractors. By creating a committee of employee, management, and union representatives, we were able to successfully identify what each group wanted to achieve. All three groups reached agreement on the issues that were key to their concerns, and conceded on smaller, less important issues. There was no time lost as a result of the negotiations and employee satisfaction rose significantly.

Tenacity

How tenacious are you? Give an example that demonstrates you at your most tenacious.
I am very tenacious, as is demonstrated by the successful merger between Next-Day Freight and Parcel Pick-Up. Parcel Pick-Up was a family business passed down through three generations and was suffering badly from the high cost of its overheads and a downturn in its specialty service—small parcel delivery. I met with the then-Managing Director in 1995 to discuss the possibility of a merger, and it was clear that he was not prepared to concede. It took almost three years of regular meetings and negotiations to build his confidence in our business. In 1998, we successfully merged, retaining all existing staff, combining support functions, and sharing overheads.

Employment History

Jones Bros., Inc.   **3/2003 to Present**
Jones Bros. is a large national company that owns a range of goods transportation systems. Next-Day Freight provides distribution systems for a broad customer base, including a range of major companies.

State Manager for Next-Day Freight, Chicago, IL

Reporting to the General Manager, major responsibilities in this position include acting as a change agent reshaping the business into a professional and profitable organization with a strong emphasis on customer service. The bottom-line responsibility of this position is a $50 million business unit employing 350 people in sales, administration, operations, marketing, customer service, quality, and security.

Major Achievements:
- Created and implemented a state business plan addressing major shortfalls in the business.
- Orchestrated a successful merger with another $10 million business unit.
- Restructured the entire sales force.
- Negotiated and implemented a new enterprise agreement.
- Directed a complete management restructure.
- Introduced new Management Information Systems.
- Negotiated the outsourcing of $2.5 million in annual casual labor.
- Coordinated the rebuilding of a major new depot facility.
- Implemented a quantifiable quality improvement program.
- Developed a new marketing strategy.

- Developed a major strategic industrial relations plan to create greater incentives for the workforce.
- Led the business unit to its best profit performance.

National Petroleum, Inc.   **2/1991 to 2/2003**
National is a major petroleum company that owns refineries throughout North America, as well as a major franchise network of automotive fuel stations.

National Distribution Network Manager, Des Moines, IA   *3/1998 to 2/2003*

Reporting to the National Planning Manager, responsible for the strategic development and network rationalization of the wholesale distribution business worth more than $80 million per year to company profit. Maintained primary trade and developed an environment for improved profit performance based on best practices, operating efficiency, and optimum capital investment.

Major Achievements:
- Performed comprehensive review of the sector and developed an integrated business plan for the next century.
- Developed a new network process to contain the best demographic mix of distribution and marketing.
- Developed and implemented a merchandising-based franchise package.
- Implemented a business planning process for independent distributors.
- Directed the strategic business review of a $300 million subsidiary.
- Managed the wholesale investment budget to achieve corporate objectives.
- Successfully rationalized and restructured the distributor business to improve the return on investment.

Regional Finance Manager, Des Moines, IA   *3/1996 to 2/1998*

Reporting to the Regional Manager, responsible for the financial performance of the dealer and distributor businesses within the area. Activity entailed the management of profitability, franchisee selection, and administration.

Senior Reseller Area Manager, Kearney, NE   *1/1995 to 2/1996*

Reporting to the Wholesale Network Development Manager, responsible for bottom-line profit, achievement of volume targets, financial management, and credit control, tendering for new business and network development.

Marketing, Planning, and Economics Officer, Kearney, NE   *2/1992 to 12/1994*

Responsible for SWOT analyses, forecasting, and preparation of cost submissions.

Transport Distribution Manager, Kearney, NE   *2/1991 to 1/1992*

Consulting to wholesale fuel distributors.

Rundle and Smith Chartered Accountants   **1/1989 to 1/1991**
Team audit work for a range of companies. Left to pursue a marketing career.

Which Resume Is for Me?

Our extensive work has found that hiring managers prefer resumes that look conventional. This has been found in studies throughout the world. Most managers are conventional people, and they have a clear idea of what they expect to see when they read a resume. Reading a resume is a bit like walking into a restaurant—we know what to expect. In a restaurant, we know that there will be tables and a menu, that we will be asked for our order, and that we will have to pay for the food. We might even expect to leave a tip! Receiving an unusual resume would be like walking into the restaurant and seeing no tables or serving staff. We might figure out that there is a food vending machine to use, or alternatively, we might just walk out. Similarly, an employer might persevere with an unusual resume, or he or she might just reject it.

Before we look at some actual examples, we will take a look at what things you should put in your resume. The following is our list of important elements of a resume.

➤ **Tip:** Use our 4-S rule: Keep it Simple, Structured, Succinct, and Significant.

Essential Contact Details

Always include your

- Name you want to be known by—for example, "James Bright" and not "James Edward Harold Bright"
- Home address
- Telephone number
- Fax number
- E-mail address

Only give contact details for places where you are prepared to be contacted by prospective employers. If receiving a call or an e-mail at your current workplace might lead to embarrassing questions from your boss, do not give work contact details. Of course, if you want to include an e-mail address, it is now very easy to get a free e-mail account on the Web from companies like Hotmail (www.hotmail.com).

You must put your name, address, and telephone number on the first page of your resume.

Education and Training

If you haven't had any formal education, obviously you omit these elements and should be thinking of using the functional or the structured interview resume. Have a look at the ideal candidate you constructed from the job ad in Chapter 4. What qualifications is our potential employer looking for? These qualifications are the ones to focus on.

➤ **Tip:** Do not bore the reader by listing every qualification you have obtained—keep it to the relevant and impressive stuff.

Go through the list of qualifications you made in Chapter 6 and determine which are relevant to the job. List the relevant ones in order. Some qualifications, like a college degree, are regarded as relevant information in most circumstances. Other qualifications, such as a first-aid course, may be seen as useful for some jobs, but would look odd being listed for others.

Although we have not researched where your educational details are best positioned, we find that what works best depends on how important and impressive your qualifications are to the position. Ask yourself the questions "How important are my qualifications to this position?" "How impressed will employers be by my degree I have or the school that I attended?" "What is most impressive, my qualifications or my work achievements?" If the answers to these questions are in favor of your educational qualifications, then place them toward the top of your resume (after the career objective statement or competencies and before your work achievements). If you answer in favor of your work achievements, then place educational details after your work details.

Our colleagues agree you should take a tailored approach to positioning details of your education where they are needed most. Wendy Enelow, co-author of the *Expert Resumes* series of resume guides, recommends that you "load" the resume—upfront—with your greatest selling points. Susan Britton Whitcomb, author of *Résumé Magic* (2003), has an excellent three-year rule of thumb for determining where to position your education. If you received a degree that is relevant to the vacancy in the last three years, place it toward the top of your resume. If you graduated more than three years ago and you have relevant work achievements to be proud of, place these first. Louise Kursmark, author of *Sales and Marketing Resumes for $100,000 Careers* and many other books, suggests that education be viewed as a foundational credential rather than as a key selling point. Remember, don't waste prime resume "real estate" on something that will never sell.

➤ **Tip:** Be clear and concise, and always refer back to the job ad to ensure that you're remaining relevant.

When you do include your educational qualifications, you should order them as follows:

- Highest postgraduate qualification—masters or Ph.D., the subject, and the university at which the degree was earned
- Highest undergraduate qualification—the degree, the subject, and the university at which the degree was earned
- College qualifications—what college you attended and your grade-point average

This point may not apply to many people at all, but should you have a Ph.D., bear in mind that the title of Ph.D. dissertations can often appear to be so obscure or trivially narrow as to detract from a great achievement. Believe us, we have heard the sniggers that sometimes accompany Ph.D. award presentation ceremonies! If you have a very specialized title that is not going to be directly relevant to the job you're applying for, stick to the subject discipline name (such as chemistry, physics, English, or psychology). For example, if you're applying for a research role, a title such as "An investigation into the antecedents and consequences of brown squirrel mating rituals" might be better referred to as "Biology"—unless you are applying for a job that requires you to specifically monitor squirrels.

If you have a degree, it is probably not necessary to include your high school results unless they are exceptional. A degree will lead most employers to credit you with a certain amount of intelligence.

What might be useful is to list a few subjects you covered in high school, to give an indication of your versatility. For instance, if you have an arts degree, it is probably worth listing "courses included mathematics, chemistry, and statistics" or other numerate subjects studied at high school, as this gives an indication of well-rounded abilities. The opposite applies to science graduates, who might list English and history if applicable. List any extra languages that you speak, but see our later section on bias.

If there is any special thesis topic or aspect of your studies that is particularly relevant to the job, mention it here. With all qualifications, do not assume that the reader will understand what they are.

If you are applying for a job in the same country and state in which you were trained, and the qualification system has not changed in the last 10 years, it is safe to assume that the employer will understand the meaning of your qualifications. Otherwise, do not assume anyone else will understand your qualifications, and if in doubt explain what they mean.

➤ **Tip:** When applying for a job in another state or country, don't assume employers will understand what your qualifications mean. Explain your grades and degrees in the employer's local system.

Your Work History

Go back to the lists that you made in Chapter 6 and try to pick out what in your work history either matches the ideal candidate you have constructed, or looks impressive in its own right.

Your work history is the most "wordy" part of the resume. This is where you have the most scope to influence the reader through your writing style, the words you use, and the way you describe yourself.

Generally, list your most recent job first, and then move on to the previous one, and so on. If you have a long work history with many different jobs, we recommend that you list full details for only the positions held in the past 10 years. If there are some earlier jobs that are particularly relevant to the application, you should include them.

For each job, you should list the following:
  • Dates (in years) of employment
  • Job title
  • Employer's name and city location if appropriate
  • Your responsibilities (keep it brief)
  • Your achievements in the job

➤ **Tip:** Tailor your resume to suit the requirements of the ad and include achievements (not just duties), because this is what will sell you.

The last point on this list is possibly one of the most important. Just providing a job description is not enough. If many applicants have similar backgrounds, the hiring manager will be bored to tears and may not even read your resume. What makes you different, and more employable, are all of your achievements.

In a study we conducted, employers were shown two resumes that were identical except that one described only duties in the job history and the other described achievements. The resume that included achievements was rated much more highly by the recruiters. They were far more impressed with the candidate.

➤ **Tip:** Always emphasize your achievements in each different job.

The following is a typical job history.

What does this
company do?

Employment History

Trinity Mutual

Executive Director, Trinity Mutual Master Trust—3/2004–Present
Key responsibilities include all aspects of the Master Trust, with 25 staff across four departments, including marketing, client administration, systems, and accounting.

President Mutual, 1990–2004   Any achievements?

Marketing Manager—2002–2003
Key responsibilities included product development and maintenance, marketing, and communications of the entire product range of the division.

Assistant General Manager, Financial Products—2001–2002
As above.

Senior Investment Manager, Operations—1997–2001
Key responsibilities included the day-to-day operations of President Funds Management and "unusual" investments, such as leveraged leases, junk bonds, etc.

Fund Manager, Life Fund and Insurance Bonds—1996–1997
Key responsibilities included managing the $3.5 billion Life Fund and the $1.5 billion Insurance Bond Fund, including asset allocation, general management, and "unusual" investments.

Fund Manager, Insurance Bonds—1993–1996
Key responsibilities included managing the new Insurance Bond Fund, including asset allocation, general management, and "unusual" investments.

Actuarial and Investment roles—1990–1993
In this period I was engaged in a number of actuarial roles and investment positions within President Mutual.

Figure 8.5: A typical job history.

The Achievement Focus

Here is the same job history, but this time there is an emphasis on achievements.

Tells you what the
company does.

Employment History

Trinity Mutual—3/2004–Present
Trinity Mutual is a major insurance agency that operates nationwide.

Executive Director, Trinity Mutual Master Trust—3/2000–Present
Key responsibilities include all aspects of the Master Trust, with 25 staff across four departments, including marketing, client administration, systems, and accounting. Major achievements included successful relocation of the administration, accounting, and systems areas from external suppliers to head office.

President Mutual—1990–2004
President Mutual is a major insurance agency that operates nationwide.

Clear set of
achievements.

Marketing Manager—2002–2003
Key responsibilities included product development and maintenance, marketing and communications of the entire product range of the division. During this time, sales rose by 14 percent, compared with a 5 percent average rise in the area.

Assistant General Manager, Financial Products—2001–2002
As above.

Senior Investment Manager, Operations—1997–2001
Key responsibilities included the day-to-day operations of President Funds Management and "unusual" investments, such as leveraged leases and junk bonds.

Fund Manager, Life Fund and Insurance Bonds—1996–1997
Key responsibilities included managing the $3.5 billion Life Fund and the $1.5 billion Insurance Bond Fund, including asset allocation, general management, and "unusual" investments. The fund outperformed all the indexes.

Fund Manager, Insurance Bonds—1993–1996
Key responsibilities included managing the new Insurance Bond Fund, including asset allocation, general management, and "unusual" investments. Major achievements included growing the Fund from $5 million to more than $1 billion.

Actuarial and investment roles—1/1990–6/1993
In this period, I was engaged in a number of actuarial roles and investment positions within President Mutual.

Figure 8.6: A job history with a focus on achievements.

Turning Responsibilities into Achievements

What achievements has this person had?

General Manager, Merchandise and Marketing

The major responsibilities in this role included the following:
- Overall accountability for the product, merchandising, and promotions for the 100 stores nationwide
- Product sourcing
- Financial control of the sales budget
- Managing the team of 12 buying and merchandising staff
- Ongoing liaison with state management
- Control of and accountability for the advertising and marketing needs of the stores

---

What would you look for? Where could achievements be emphasized? The first thing to catch the eye is the overall accountability for 100 stores. Can the applicant point to any financial improvements in the stores' performance? What about the sourcing of the products—any reduction in costs there, or sources of novel products?

The job is a coordinating role—is there any evidence of achievements in organizing the systems the applicant controls? Did the applicant introduce any new marketing strategies or just carry on where the predecessor left off? (That is, did they show initiative?)

The above description could be enhanced by referring directly to achievements that answer these questions. Remember, your resume is supposed to answer questions, not raise them in the minds of the recruiter.

The improved version is shown below.

General Manager, Merchandise and Marketing

The major responsibilities in this role included:
- Overall accountability for the product, merchandising, and promotions for the 100 stores across the nation
- Product sourcing
- Financial control of the sales budget
- Managing the team of 12 buying and merchandising staff
- Ongoing liaison with state management
- Control and accountability of the advertising and marketing needs of the stores

---

Major achievements included:
- Restructuring the buying department, resulting in increased productivity and lower costs
- Changes to the supply chain, resulting in a four percent increase in margins
- Development of reporting systems, resulting in enhanced financial planning
- Introduction of new offshore merchandise resources
- Development and implementation of marketing strategies
- Involvement in new stores and refurbishments
- Establishment of quality management functions

You can see that adding the major achievements gives a much more favorable impression of the applicant.

So what constitutes an achievement? Here is our list of criteria for job-related achievements:

- Completing something successfully
- An outcome that can be attributed in at least part to you
- Something that is measurable (profits, turnover, savings, words per minute)
- Something that you can prove to have happened or can be verified
- Making a change or a difference

Examples of achievements are
- Winning a customer service award
- Improving profits
- Introducing a profitable product
- Increasing the number of cars serviced per week
- Reducing the number of customer complaints
- Reducing the turnaround time for orders
- Increasing the reliability of a service

You have now rewritten your resume using more positive language, emphasizing all your achievements. So it's time to see whether what you have passes the resume fitness test!

Remember from Chapter 3 how employers think about "fit" in terms of knowledge, skills, abilities, and attitudes? Have you figured out
- What experience is required for the job
- The skills needed to do the job
- The abilities that will be required
- The sort of person/attitudes the employer expects?

Regarding you, have you included on your resume the following:
- Relevant knowledge
- Relevant skills
- Demonstrated compatible abilities
- Demonstrated compatible attitudes?

If your resume passes the fitness test, you should now apply our Gestalt test!

The Gestalt Rules of Resumes

This set of rules comes from the respected Gestalt branch of psychology. These well-established rules were used to describe visual perception, but they apply equally well to resumes.

1. **Similarity:** People will group together as roughly the same, similar jobs and experiences.
2. **Grouping:** People will assume things that are close together belong together. In other words, if you were in a team that had a success, that would put you close to a success and the success would be associated with you.
3. **Closure:** People look for closure on projects and activities—can you demonstrate that you finished projects you started?
4. **Continuity:** People will assume that things that follow closely in a similar pattern are part of a longer-term logical development.

Similarity

You can use this rule effectively on your resume. By emphasizing the similarity of your previous jobs to the one you are applying for, you increase the fit between you and the job. Equally, similarity may govern which jobs to include and which to leave out of a resume. If you have a long work history, it may be sensible to concentrate on listing only those jobs that you have done in the past 5 to 10 years, especially if these are the most similar to the one you are going for.

Here is an example of the similarity effect:

Employment History
1989–90: Receptionist, Blue Blot Ink Co.
1990–92: Secretary, Blue Blot Ink Co.
1992–98: Sales Assistant, Jeans R Us
1998–99: Secretary, Hercules Music Company
1999–2005: Call Center Operator, Big Brick Phone Co.
2005–06: Personal Assistant to CEO, Big Brick Phone Co.
2006–Present: Personal Assistant to CEO, Slender Phones, Inc.

What skills would you describe this person as having? Most people would get the impression from this history that the candidate was a secretary. This is because the terms "receptionist," "secretary," and "personal assistant" all conjure up ideas of similar jobs, whereas "sales assistant" and "call center operator" seem dissimilar. The power of this effect can be seen when you add up the number of years doing the various jobs. This person spent more time (12 years out of 20) *not* being a secretary!

Closure

Closure is something that many employers will be looking for. They want to see that you can see things through, and that you don't quit when the going gets tough. Can you give examples where you completed a project successfully at work? Closure can also be demonstrated by showing that you moved to the next job because your work was completed in the old job, or that you had gained all the personal development you could expect:

> "I moved on because I needed a new challenge, having mastered my old job."

Grouping

This is a powerful effect. If you were "close" to some outcome, you will be associated with it. It is a bit like being at the scene of the crime—you automatically become one of the witnesses (and sometimes a suspect).
Consider the following two work histories.

Negative Grouping

> I started in the commodities team and moved on to sales when the team was disbanded. The sales were outsourced in 1995, when I joined the merchant division.

Positive Grouping

> I was part of the commodities team that broke all the market records, and then moved to sales, where the group achieved a 25 percent improvement. This led to my current position in the merchant division.

You can see the power of grouping well here. The first example gives the impression of a loser and the second gives the impression of a winner, despite the lack of evidence to suggest the candidate was responsible either for any of the successes or failures.

Continuity

This relates most obviously to gaps in career history. We will spend some more time considering this later. However, it is worth pointing out here that most employers want to see continuity of employment. Continuity has two aspects. Firstly, have you been continuously employed over the years; and, secondly, does your work history combine to tell a logical story, or does it appear random? The following examples illustrate this point:

Continuous Employment but Discontinuous Types of Jobs

1989–90: Receptionist, Blue Blot Ink Co.

1990–92: Assistant Chemist, Blue Blot Ink Co.

1992–98: Sales Assistant, Jeans R Us

1998–99: Product Packer, Hercules Music Company

1999–2005: Stores Administrator, Big Brick Phone Co.

2005–06: Sales Representative, Big Brick Phone Co.

2006–Present: Glazier, Heritage Doors, Inc.

Continuous Employment and Reasonably Continuous Types of Jobs

1989–90: Receptionist, Blue Blot Ink Co.

1990–92: Secretary, Blue Blot Ink Co.

1992–98: Sales Assistant, Jeans R Us

1998–99: Secretary, Hercules Music Company

1999–2005: Call Center Operator, Big Brick Phone Co.

2005–06: Personal Assistant to CEO, Big Brick Phone Co.

2006–Present: Personal Assistant to CEO, Slender Phones, Inc.

From these examples, you can see clearly that the story of the first candidate's working life is a very confused and mixed one. It doesn't create a great impression. The second candidate's history tells a story of steady advancement (and therefore achievement) in the secretarial area. It is a much more positive story.

Now that you know all about the Gestalt laws, use them to guide what goes into your resume and what does not, how to word your job history, and how to present your resume. Once your resume passes the fitness test and the Gestalt test, you are ready to put the icing on the cake! In the next chapter, we discuss some more techniques that our research has demonstrated to be effective.

Presenting Your Resume

In this chapter, you will learn how to
- *Set up your resume for maximum effect*
- *Use bullet points or continuous prose where appropriate*

We have already touched on some basic points about the best way to present your resume—we've seen that simple typefaces and plain white paper are preferred by recruiters. In this chapter, we look at successful presentation in more detail.

Layout—The Sections Your Resume Should Include

The first thing to say about the layout of your resume is do not put the words "Resume" or "Curriculum Vitae" on the top of your resume. Quite apart from insulting the reader—what else could the document be?—it is a waste of valuable space.

Contact Information

At the top of the first page of your resume, put your name (or the name you wish to be known by). It should be in bold type, at a size of 16 points, centered on the page. Leave plenty of white space below this heading, before you list your personal contact details. Aligned on the left side of the page, give your address. Use the right side on the same lines to give your telephone and fax numbers.

The Rest of the Resume

The remainder of your resume appears in the following order:

- Summary or job objective statement
- Work history
- Education details (although there are variations on this)
- Professional associations
- References (if you include them) come last, or go on a separate sheet

Section Heading Style

The main headings have to be consistent in appearance. They must all be the same font and size. In Figure 9.4, there are three different levels of headings. The applicant's name is in Arial, 16 points in size, and is in bold. The major sections "Education" and "Work History" are 14 points and bold. Subheadings under "Work History" are in 12-point type, and the text is 12- or 11-point Arial.

Making the same type of headings look the same is another example of the Gestalt law of similarity. The reader finds it easy to see the separate sections when the headings are formatted consistently.

White Space and Grouping

You must leave plenty of white space on your resume. If you put too much writing on a page, your resume will be hard to read and look cluttered. You should also allow a generous margin of at least 1 inch on all sides. White space can be used to apply the Gestalt principle of grouping (that things close to each other belong together). In the example, there is plenty of space between the person's contact details and their education. There are smaller gaps between their college and degrees, and then there is a larger gap again between the education and the work history. The size of the gaps tells the reader that the things close together are all related. The larger gap indicates to the reader that they are moving on to some different type of information.

Fonts

Use the same font for the body text throughout; here are some good examples of fonts to use:

> ✔ The fast cat jumped over the lazy dog. (Arial)
> ✔ The fast cat jumped over the lazy dog. (Times New Roman)
> ✔ The fast cat jumped over the lazy dog. (Tahoma)
> ✔ The fast cat jumped over the lazy dog. (Palatino)

Figure 9.1: These are acceptable fonts for your resume.

Here are some fonts you should not use:

> ✗ The fast cat jumped over the lazy dog. (Comic Sans MS)
> ✗ *The fast cat jumped over the lazy dog.* (Brush Script)
> ✗ The fast cat jumped over the lazy dog. (Chiller)

Figure 9.2: Don't use fonts like these!

Text Formatting: Bullet Points or Continuous Prose?

We did some research to see whether recruiters had a preference for work histories presented in bullet points or as continuous prose (that is, as a series of normal sentences). The results were not straightforward. Recruiters tended to prefer candidates to write complete sentences, but if the resume had been rewritten by a recruitment agency, they tended to prefer bullet points!

So what should you do?

Bullet points are quick and easy to read, and look attractive on the page, as long as there are not too many of them. The risk with bullet points is that people tend to be too brief and the bullet point becomes meaningless. For example:

> Good working knowledge of Word and Excel and some experience with PowerPoint.

Compare this with

> • Word, Excel, PowerPoint.

The first sentence provides more information than the bullet.

➤ **Tip:** If you are going to use bullet points, make sure that they are meaningful.

Finally, it is worth noting that writing complete sentences allows you to show off your communication skills if your spelling and grammar are good.

Other Important Layout and Presentation Issues

Here are some other points to keep in mind:

- You should not underline headings. It tends to look messy, and headings may also be misread by computer scanners. (Refer to Chapter 17 for more about this.)
- Do not use both sides of the paper. People may forget to photocopy or scan both sides.
- You must have your resume laser-printed. Using old or cheaper printers is not acceptable now that high-quality laser printers are commonly available.
- Do not use color on your resume. It often looks tacky and cannot be photocopied easily.
- Do not put clip art, cartoons, or other illustrations on your resume. (Remember our advice about wacky resumes?)
- Use high-quality paper that is white (other colors may not scan or copy well).
- If you are sending out photocopies, ensure that the quality of the copy is excellent (a good copy is almost indistinguishable from an original).
- Do not fold your resume—buy an 8½ × 11 envelope.

Before-and-After Resume Example

The following is an example of poorly laid-out resume, followed by the same resume with much better layout.

Confidential Resume of:

Name: Ian Gregory Chappell
Address: 3360 Edgecliff Avenue, Seattle, WA 98101
Telephone: (206) 555-5555
(206) 123-4567 (work)
Fax: (206) 444-4545 (work)
e-mail: igchappell@hotmail.com

Work History

1998–2003   **Optus, Seattle, WA**
                                           An international telecommunications company

         Communications Engineer
         Was responsible…

         Senior Communications Manager
         Performed…

2003–Present   **Telstra, Seattle, WA**
         Operations Manager
         Currently responsible for…

Education

St. Mark of the Blessed Taylor High School, Redmond, WA
B.S., Electrical Engineering, University of Washington, 1994, *summa cum laude*

Figure 9.3: A resume with poor layout

Ian Gregory Chappell

3360 Edgecliff Avenue
Seattle, WA 98101
igchappell@hotmail.com

(206) 555-5555 (home)
(206) 123-4568 (cell)
Fax: (206) 444-4545

Work History

Telstra, Seattle, WA   **2003–Present**

Operations Manager
Currently responsible for...

Optus, Seattle, WA   **1998–2003**
An international telecommunications company.

Communications Engineer
Responsible for...

Senior Communications Manager
Performed...

Education

B.S., Electrical Engineering, University of Washington, 1994, *summa cum laude*

Figure 9.4: A resume with good layout.

Anatomy of an Effective Layout

Which of the following resume layouts looks the best?

Resume 1

Resume 2

Resume 3

Figure 9.5: Sample resume layouts.

Figure 9.5, continued.

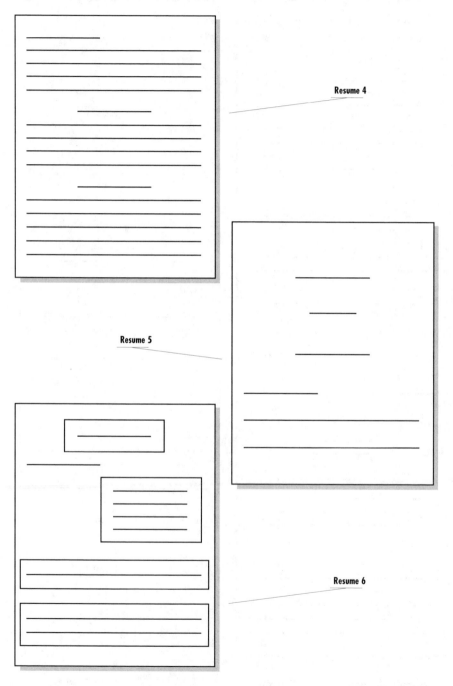

We think the outstanding winner is Resume 2. The layout achieves a nice balance between the amount of information provided and the overall neat-and-tidy, easy-to-read appearance. Secondly, this resume has used the Gestalt proximity rule ("things that are close together will be assumed to belong together"). In Resume 2, although you cannot read the writing, you can clearly see the different sections. This makes the resume look more logical and structured—and we cannot even read what it is saying! Notice how this resume leaves larger margins at the top and bottom and on the left and right.

Resume 3 is not too bad, although the structure is a little less clear. Ideally, the resume should have definite sections—name, contact details, summary or objective, job history/skills, training/education. On this resume, it looks as though the name and contact details are all bunched together.

Resume 1 is not too bad, but notice how your eye is drawn to the empty white space at the top right. It looks as though a photograph or picture has been removed. This layout might be a good idea if you are submitting an electronic resume or if you think that the resume is likely to be scanned into a computer. The alignment of the text on the left, and the fact that each new section starts at the left margin makes it less likely that a computer will misread your resume. (See Chapter 17 for more on formatting electronic resumes.)

Resume 5 is an example of taking the idea of "white space" a bit too far. Here the resume looks like it contains very little information, and it suggests either that the candidate has little to offer, or that we are in for about 10 pages of artistic minimalism!

Resumes 4 and 6 are shockers! Resume 4 is an example of what happens when the writer has not thought through what they want to say and therefore attempts to cram in as much as possible. Remember, less can often be more with resumes. The look of this resume is off-putting and suggests to the reader that they might need a sack lunch to help them get all the way through it! This layout can be justified only when the resume is being used for a proposal where a very strict page limit on the overall application is demanded, or perhaps where a candidate has been specifically asked (perhaps after an interview) to provide a much more detailed background document. For everyone else, if your resume resembles Resume 4, it should be rewritten immediately!

Resume 6 is a mess. The boxes around the text are distracting, and although they clearly indicate the various different sections, the same effect can be achieved in a less heavy-handed manner with judicious use of white space (as in Resume 2). Furthermore, these boxes may throw off a computer scan of the resume. Resist the temptation to show off your skills with using the Draw or Insert Picture commands on your word processor.

The Icing on the Cake

So now you have a resume, beautifully laid out and crammed with achievements. You've baked your cake! Next, we show you how to improve your resume even further, by putting the icing on the cake. In this section, we explore the techniques that have been shown by our research to be successful in impressing recruiters.

CHAPTER 10

Mind Your Language!

In this chapter, you will learn
- *That language matters on a resume*
- *Which words can enhance a resume*
- *Which words and phrases can detract from a resume*

We have spent a lot of time discussing just how important it is to emphasize your results and successes on your resume, but this should not be at the expense of making sure the language on your resume is absolutely perfect.

Word Power

When you list your achievements, pay attention to how you write about them. The words you choose can have a huge influence on employers. Employers will judge your resume on how well you communicate, so choosing the right words is very important. Think back to the beginning when we were discussing the importance of selling yourself. The following verbs are examples of good "selling" words:

overcame	achieved	enlarged	developed	discovered
controlled	managed	delivered	reorganized	won
applied	defeated	eliminated	engineered	overhauled
presented	founded	instigated	created	directed
attracted	led	initiated	established	succeeded
contributed	modified	specialized	expanded	repaired
improved	analyzed	coordinated	trained	organized
guided	conducted	implemented	built	designed
persuaded	helped	proved	utilized	simplified
investigated	completed	compiled	demonstrated	accomplished
transformed	introduced	finalized	headed	built
supervised	illustrated	outlined	selected	monitored

You can boost the power of your selling verbs even more by adding power adjectives, such as the following:

quickly	successfully	rapidly	carefully	decisively
competently	resourcefully	capably	efficiently	consistently
effectively	positively	cooperatively	selectively	creatively
assertively	energetically	enthusiastically	responsibly	flexibly

Words with negative connotations should be avoided if possible. Here are some examples of negative words to avoid:

avoided	failed	succumbed	relied	conflicted
tried	disciplined	attempted	abandoned	unsuccessfully
lost	dismissed	withdrew	relinquished	argued

➤ **Tip:** Write positively. It's all about attitude!

Clichés

When writing and editing your resume, beware of clichés. Clichés are overused phrases that become meaningless and irritating. For instance, "Have a nice day," or "in the blink of an eye," or "the end of the world," or "Make my day." Unfortunately, the world of work has a peculiar love of clichés, so it is difficult to know when you are "going overboard" (to use a cliché). For example, avoid using phrases such as

- Mission-critical
- Blue-sky
- Out of the box
- Cutting-edge
- Seamless
- Team player
- Big picture
- Win-win

➤ **Tip:** Avoid putting clichés in your resume. At best, they will disregarded; at worst, they will irritate the reader.

Here a few examples of business clichés that are still okay to use:

- Total quality. Beware not to overuse this term (for example, total added value, or total global communication, etc.—or the word "quality").
- Added value. (Yuck! But some people appear to like it.)
- Global
- Downsizing
- Rightsizing
- Outsourcing
- Focus (as in "customer focus" or "team focus"…but not "total focus")

Now read through your list of achievements and look closely at each word you have used. Is there another word that might make you look more impressive? If so, replace the word with the more positive one.

Technical Language

Many jobs in the legal, medical, scientific, and computing areas have lots of jargon words associated with them. It is always very difficult to know when and where to use such words. You can be sure it is safe to use words or phrases that appear in the job advertisement or description. If the employer uses simplified words or phrases to describe some technical aspect of a job, then you should also stick to the simplified words. However, in this case it is permissible to provide more technical examples to illustrate your point.

For instance, if the advertisement says "high-level statistical knowledge required," it is permissible to include a statement such as "I have a very high level of statistical knowledge, including the use of multiple regression, analysis of variance, and structural equation modeling techniques." The first part of the sentence uses the same language as the advertisement, and second part goes into more detail. If you had only included the second part of the sentence, it is possible that the person reading the resume initially might not have the technical knowledge to appreciate that "multiple regression, analysis of variance, and structural equation modeling techniques" are high-level statistical techniques, so your resume might have been rejected.

Remember that there is a fundamental imbalance between the applicant and the employer at this stage. It is permissible for the employer to use jargon terms that send you to the library seeking clarification, but do not be tempted to throw your own different jargon back at them—employers do not want to visit the library!

Some useful texts and Web sites that can assist you in simplifying your language for a general audience include the following:

- *Chicago Manual of Style,* 15th Edition
- *The Elements of Style*
- www.webopedia.com
- www.acronymfinder.com
- *Merriam Webster Collegiate Dictionary,* Tenth Edition

CHAPTER 11

Using Competency Statements

In this chapter, you will learn
- *What a competency statement is*
- *How to construct a competency statement*
- *How to increase your job "fit" by using competency statements*

What Is a Competency Statement?

Put simply, a competency statement briefly outlines the knowledge, skills, attitudes, and abilities you possess. Think back to Chapter 2 where we talked about "fit." We showed you how employers think about jobs in terms of the knowledge, skills, attitude, and abilities required to do the job.

A competency statement should address all these points, and should serve to increase the perception of fit between you and the job in the employer's mind.

➤ **Tip:** Include competency statements in your resume and back them up with examples.

Here are some example statements created to emphasize some quality that an employer is seeking:

- **Highly motivated:** Proven track record of achievement, both in college and through extracurricular activities. Won numerous awards throughout academic career while maintaining a balance with social activities.
- **Sales market knowledge:** In touch with the market through sales journals and magazines, as well as visits to supermarkets and other points of

sale. Completed the research project "What Makes a Supermarket Tick: Best Placement or Best Product?," which looked at the dynamics of product placement in stores and the impact on sales.

- **Organizational skills:** Excellent organizational skills developed to ensure effective time management, maximum output in minimum time, and the ability to handle a number of activities simultaneously.
- **Energetic:** A person who is always on the go; involved in a number of activities ranging from academic to work-related to sporting activities, particularly team sports. An outgoing person who enjoys being an active member of numerous clubs and associations.
- **Communication skills:** Diverse range of experiences in college, at work, and in extracurricular activities has fostered strong verbal and written communication skills. An outgoing person, who has also had numerous opportunities to develop interpersonal skills to a high level.
- **Responsible:** Involved in a range of activities, developing a responsible and mature approach to any task undertaken or situation.

You can see from looking at all the statements that each one addresses one aspect of a job. The words in bold are the words that the candidate has realized are critical components of the job from analyzing the job advertisement.

Here is a job advertisement with the keywords in bold:

Entry-Level Sales Analyst
Transform your career!

Step up to an organization that's **on the move globally,** with consumer and pharmaceutical products that consistently set a new standard for excellence at the world-class level.

As a crucial member of our Household Products sales team, you will be working with leading brands. Your exceptional analytical ability will enable you to analyze market data, and **working closely with Account Managers,** help build our brands in the marketplace.
Carefully monitoring sales of our products and our competitors' products will be of prime importance. You will be more than just a "number cruncher" in this role—you will develop an intimate understanding of how the grocery trade operates: both from the retailer's and the manufacturers' perspective.

We're looking for a person who is **motivated, in touch with the marketplace,** and who can ably provide tactical support in achieving specific objectives. Requirement for the position is a college degree in business, marketing, or a related discipline. You may have some sales or retail experience and a strong desire to pursue a **sales** career. A track record of **achievement** is essential!

Figure 11.1: A sample job advertisement with bold keywords.

You can see from an analysis of the advertisement what sort of qualities this company is looking for in the job:

- "On the move globally" means they want someone who is energetic
- "working closely with Account Managers" means the candidate will need communication and organization skills

- "Carefully monitoring" means they want someone who is responsible
- "Motivated" and "achievement" mean that they want someone who is highly motivated
- "In touch with the marketplace" means that you must have sales market knowledge.

The competency statement for each quality is simply a short sentence or two saying why you have those qualities. You can see how these sorts of statements emphasize the fit between the candidate and job more directly than a mere job history can.

Do They Work?

We were not at all convinced that such statements would be effective, but were amazed to find that, when we included them on resumes, they boosted our candidates' chances by as much as 30 percent. In one study, a candidate whose resume did not include these statements was not selected for an interview by any of our professional recruiters and HR professionals. When we put competency statements on the resume, one in three recruiters said they would interview the candidate! For another candidate, when the statements were included on the resume, every hiring authority said they would interview the candidate, whereas only eight out of ten said they would interview the candidate when the statements were missing.

We were so surprised by these results that we did another study to check whether we had made a mistake. We got *exactly* the same results.

> **Tip:** Always include as much quantifiable data as possible when listing achievements.

Where Should You Put Competency Statements on a Resume?

We have tried placing these statements at the end of the resume, and we have placed them at the beginning after the applicant's name. We've put them on the second page, and we've put them in the cover letter, all with exactly the same results. It does not seem to matter where you put them, as long as they are there. We usually put them under the heading "Knowledge, Skills, and Abilities."

Why Do Competency Statements Work?

There are probably several reasons why they are so successful. Firstly, you are picking up on the attributes the employer thinks are important and addressing each of them—it's a bit like answering an interview question such as "Tell me, do you have any sales market knowledge?" You are talking the employer's language.

Secondly, you are making it easier for the employer to see the fit between you and the job because you have taken the trouble to point out all the things you have in common. It may also make give a computer scanner more keywords to pick out.

Finally, the very fact that you've put this extra section on your resume shows you have thought a bit more deeply about the job and how you would fit it well. It makes you stand out from all those candidates who just list their skills and qualifications as if to say "take it or leave it."

Are They a Bit Over the Top?

Very probably yes, but it doesn't seem to matter. In fact, we found that the more competency statements we included on a resume, the more likely it was that the candidate was chosen for an interview!

I Bet This "Trick" Doesn't Fool Experienced Hiring Managers!

Yes and no. While it is true that younger or inexperienced recruiters are most likely to be influenced by these statements, we found even older and very experienced recruiters tended to favor resumes containing these statements more often than standard resumes.

How Do You Write a Competency Statement?

First revisit Chapter 4, which tells you how to analyze a job advertisement. Then follow these easy steps:

1. Pick out the key qualities that the employer is looking for from the job ad. Qualities listed in Chapter 4 such as "dynamic," "great communicator," and so forth are common.
2. Go back through the achievement worksheets in Chapter 6. How can you demonstrate these desired qualities? Take a look at the example competency statements earlier in this chapter for some ideas on how to do it.

3. Carefully read through what you've written. Can you justify what you are claiming? If not, omit the statement—it is not acceptable to lie. If you are found out (which is likely), you could be fired from the job you get. Does the statement look really weak or unexceptional? If it does, omit it or strengthen it by giving concrete examples. Examples of statements that are probably too weak include "get along well with people" (strengthen by giving examples) and " a likeable person" (strengthen by giving examples). If you're having trouble coming to terms with this idea, look at the sample resumes in Chapter 15. These outline the types of competency statements to use in more detail.

The more competency statements you put on your resume, the more chance you have of being interviewed (see Table 11.1 for help writing competency statements).

Table 11.1: Competency Checklist

	Competency 1	Competency 2
What did you do?		
What was the context?		
How do you know it was successful?		
Does it convince the reader beyond a shadow of a doubt?		

Here's an example of how to use the preceding checklist. Say that the competency you list is "Outstanding Communication Skills." Here are the answers you might give for each question in the worksheet:

- **What did you do?** Provided exceptionally clear communications in my role as marketing manager, which resulted in winning several customer service awards and also a human resources award.
- **What was the context?** Provided succinct written newsletters to all staff in the division containing information about corporate goals and divisional performance, and highlighting personal achievements. Gave regular presentations and briefings to senior management on strategic planning and performance matters.
- **How do you know it was successful?** The awards I received were voted on by my colleagues in two cases, and by senior management in association with the Human Resources Association, in one case demonstrating the quality of my communication skills across a broad range of clients.
- **Does it convince the reader?** (Well, you the reader might want to judge that, but the statements contain claims that relate to the key competency "communication skills" as well as information about the context in which the competency was performed and evidence of ultimate success of the behavior demonstrated by receipt of awards!)

Using Career Objectives and Career Summary Statements

In this chapter, you will learn
- *What a career objective statement is*
- *Whether career objective statements work*
- *How to write a career objective statement*

What Is a Career Objective Statement?

A trend on resumes has been to include a career objective at the beginning of your resume. The career objective is a succinct statement that describes what type of job you want. It allows the reader to get a quick idea of your suitability for the job advertised, and it also serves to make you appear more motivated.

Career objectives can be as simple as stating what sort of job you are looking for. For instance, someone in the medical world might write the following:

> Employment in a hospital specializing in care of the elderly.

These sorts of statements have their uses in letting the reader know quickly whether you are a serious contender for the job. However, if the person in this example would also be happy caring for young children, they may be narrowing their opportunities unnecessarily. Such statements might also be seen by the reader as rather obvious. (After all, they have applied for the job!)

A good career statement might read like this:

> Accounts manager in a growing organization where I can use my communication skills to help a variety of clients.

The statement is positive, it doesn't sound too desperate (in the way that a statement like "To work for your organization" does), and it is not too limited.

A bad career statement might start like this:

> All I've ever wanted to be was...

The statement above is a real example, and gives the impression of very limited ambition and narrow focus.

It is sometimes better to see the career objective as an opportunity to market yourself as well as stating what you want to do. The following example shows how you can slip in some positive comments about your skill levels and motivation:

> A position as training manager in a progressive multinational company where I can maximize the use of my communication and teaching skills and where I will be continually challenged and stretched.

Do They Work?

A lot of people get terribly self-conscious about using these sorts of statements. However, in a study we did with recruiters, we found resumes that included career objectives influenced recruiters to think the applicants were more suited to the job they had applied for. So, yes, they do work and you should consider including one on your resume.

Career objectives probably become less effective the more experienced you are. They are certainly a good idea for young applicants, new graduates, and people in the first five or so years of their working career. They may also be a good option for people looking at changing careers.

As the name implies, they should be statements about your desired career, so they are not really appropriate for temporary jobs such as summer jobs. "To develop my skills in waiting tables…" doesn't sound quite right.

Career Objective Don'ts

Career objectives should not read like a statement of demands in a lawsuit or divorce proceedings. A good salesperson doesn't try to sell you something by saying "I want you to shut up and just hand over the asking price without negotiation or any other irritating questions." Rather, they figure out what they think you are looking for and try to offer that to you. The good salesperson might say "I want to give you total satisfaction using my excellent listening skills and superior product knowledge, and I want you to help me by letting me know what you want."

So with career objectives, focus on what you can offer the employer.

Career Summaries

For job hunters with a lot of work experience or a well-established career, the career objective can seem a little naive or unduly submissive. In this case, you should use a Career Summary instead. A Career Summary is a pitch to St. Peter to admit you into career heaven! It is a short (three to six sentences) statement summarizing a career of uninterrupted success and achievement that ends pointing unambiguously and persuasively toward the role you are applying for.

Here are two examples that Jim might use on his resume. Decide for yourself which is the good and which is the poor example.

Career Summary

Among a rapidly diminishing coterie of friends my work has been described as merely adequate. What can I say about my career that has not been covered by the Warren Commission? My work has been spread over many fields...like manure. When you think of career advisors in America, two or three names immediately spring to mind. And while you are trying to think of those, let me introduce myself...

Career Summary

A leading career advisor with extensive international recognition and sales. With more than 15 years of psychological experience, all the key areas of coaching, counseling, training, and assessment have provided many outstanding successes. With particular strengths in training and communication, the next step in my career will provide opportunities to provide strategic guidance in the development of the next generation of career coaches.

CHAPTER 13

Cover Letters

In this chapter, you will learn
- *How to write an effective cover letter*
- *Why tailoring your letter to the employer is important*

What Is a Cover Letter For?

All resumes should be accompanied by a cover letter. The cover letter has several purposes:

- It lets administrative staff know quickly what the correspondence is about.
- It is often the first thing an employer reads.
- It allows you to say why you are applying.
- It sets the tone for the resume.

Many authors seem to suggest you should produce fairly standard resumes and put your efforts into tailoring the cover letter. We do not think this is the best approach, and it should be clear that we believe you should tailor the resume for each job. One very sound reason for this is that it is the resume that usually gets more attention, and generally it is the resume (not the cover letter) that is used as the basis for questions asked in employment interviews.

➤ **Tip:** Do not think that a "one-size-fits-all" approach to your resume can be compensated for by a cover letter.

Nonetheless, you should still take cover letters seriously. You should be sure to include the essential details the employer wants to see, and make sure the letter is free of errors.

Cover Letter Rules

Here are the basic guidelines for writing a cover letter to accompany your resume:
- You must write a new one for each resume you send.
- The addressee must be correct—do not forget to change the address and salutation if you are sending the same letter to several recipients.
- The date must be correct.
- Cover letters should never be more than one page long.
- They should be as well laid out as your resume is. They should even use the same fonts, layout, and paper as your resume.
- Unless a handwritten response is specifically asked for (which is rare), you should type your letters.

➤ **Tip:** Do not state information in the cover letter that can be obtained from reading your resume. Use your cover letter to briefly summarize your qualifications and pique the employer's interest to read your resume.

What to Include in Your Letter

Your letter should include the following information:
- Your (typed) name, address, and phone number
- The name of the person to whom you are writing (get this from the job advertisement, or phone the company and ask who you should address the letter to). Always try to get a name to address the letter to. Sometimes, however, it will be impossible to find out. Here a "Dear Sir/Madam" or "Dear Hiring Manager" will have to suffice.
- Their job title
- Their address
- The initial greeting (for example, "Dear Ms. Smith,")
- The first sentence, which should state the following:
  - The job you are applying for
  - The reference number (if known)
  - Where you saw the opening advertised

- A couple of sentences that are catchy statements such as those we developed as competency statements in Chapter 11 ("I have more than five years of experience as a machinist with Bloggs and Bloggs, and have experience with a wide variety of pattern techniques.").
- A couple of sentences about why you are right for this employer/job
- A polite request for a reply or an interview
- Your signature and your name typed below it

A Cover Letter Example

The following example will give you a guide.

Ms Jenny Halse
15 Castle Street
Kingman, AZ 86403
jhalse@royal.net
(963) 222-2222

July 20, 2006

Mr. Robert Wayne
Manufacturing Manager
Laughing Boy Dog Toys
2 Rover Way
Surprise, AZ 86666

Dear Mr. Wayne,

I wish to apply for the position of Machinist (ref 0720/06) that was advertised in *The Sedona Age* on Saturday, July 20, 2006.

I have more than five years of experience as a Machinist with Weaveanduck and have knowledge of a wide variety of pattern techniques. My technical skills are second to none and I have an excellent record as a reliable, productive employee.

I will bring to this role enthusiasm, loyalty, reliability, a great team attitude, and a commitment to provide the highest possible quality in all of my work.

I am looking for new challenges, and the position of Machinist sounds like the perfect opportunity. Your organization has an enviable record in innovation in machining and an excellent reputation as an employer, making the position even more attractive.

I enclose my resume for your consideration and look forward to hearing from you soon. I am available for an interview at your convenience.

Yours sincerely,

Jenny Halse

Figure 13.1: Sample cover letter.

The Doctor Is In—Your Problems Solved

▶ ▶ ▶ ▶ ▶ ▶ ▶ ▶ ▶ ▶ *At this stage, you have put together a strong resume, and you have given it a shine and extra polish. But still you have those nagging questions about particular aspects of the resume. We hope this part of the book will answer these questions for you.*

Addressing Selection Criteria

In this chapter you will learn
- *How to decode selection criteria*
- *How selection criteria affect your resume presentation*

Selection criteria are a written list of job requirements that candidates must demonstrate that they meet before being selected for an interview. Selection criteria are a really big deal and should not be confused with the usual hyperbole found in most job advertisements. They are extremely common, and often mandatory across most public-sector jobs, including state and federal government, education, and other jobs in the public realm. These criteria are normally included in job ads or in more detailed job or position descriptions on the company's Web site. Sometimes the employer is vague about selection criteria, and we cover this in more detail in Chapter 4. Failure to explicitly and fully address selection criteria can (and very often will) lead to automatic rejection, no matter what your individual merits may be. As we said, they are a big deal and need to be taken seriously.

Selection criteria are statements that set out fairly precisely the sorts of qualities, experience, training, and behaviors (in other words, the knowledge, skills, abilities, and attitudes) that the employer seeks for the position. Employers believe that these statements help them sort out the strong candidates from the weak. Further, they are supposed to encourage employers to rank applicants based only on job-relevant criteria and therefore reduce prejudice and bias that comes from employers making judgments about a candidate's race, gender, age, attractiveness, and so on.

Here's the good news. What we've talked about in relation to analyzing job ads and writing competency statements will come in very handy in addressing selection criteria.

Deciphering the Components of a Selection Criterion

These are the most common components of selection criteria statements:

- **Competency:** This is a work-related attribute much like the competency statements in Chapter 11. This includes things like communication skills, teamwork, leadership, and ability to meet deadlines.
- **Qualifier:** This sets the level of performance a company requires and puts boundaries on what they are asking for; for instance, whether they want "advanced" accounting knowledge, or merely an "appreciation of" of accounting practices. Other terms are commonly used, such as "superior," "excellent," "outstanding," "strong," "demonstrated," "background in," "experience of," "ability to," and "understanding of."
- **Behavior:** This usually puts into context where and how the competency has to be demonstrated.
- **Importance:** There are sometimes two main categories: essential and desirable. "Essential" means that you *must* demonstrate that you meet this criterion to be selected for an interview. No manner of excuses or obfuscation will get you around a failure to address essential criteria. "Desirable" does not mean that these criteria are the most important; rather, the opposite. It means that failure to address this criterion will not automatically lead to rejection, but candidates who can demonstrate they meet the desirable criteria are likely to be ranked higher and are more likely to be interviewed. Always try to demonstrate that you possess the desirable criteria where at all possible.

Not all statements will include all these components. For instance, some statements will not refer directly to behavior, others might not include the qualifier, and so on.

Here is a typical set of criteria dissected into its components.

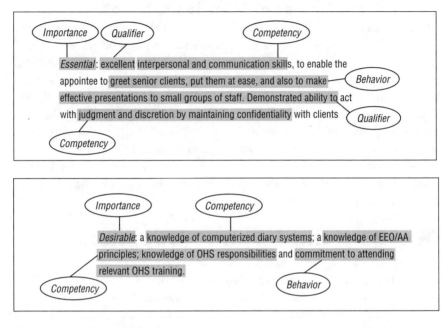

Figure 14.1: Sample selection criteria.

Decoding the Jargon—Competencies

The competencies contained in most selection criteria are usually the same as those found in general job ads (teamwork, leadership, communication skills, attention to detail, and so on). See Chapter 11 for details of the most common competency statements and what they mean.

Some competency statements elevate jargon to a more prominent role, which you cannot ignore. Common examples here include knowledge of EEO/AA principles, knowledge of OH&S policies and responsibilities, and advanced computer literacy. The first two examples refer to the organizations' policies in respect to Equal Employment Opportunity, Affirmative Action, and Occupational Health and Safety. The last example calls for a high level of familiarity and skill using a range of software programs. Generally "Advanced" computer skills mean you can use all of the basic office "productivity" software such as Microsoft Word (word processor), Excel (spreadsheet), Outlook (e-mail), and Explorer (Web browser). In addition, you would either be expected to use these programs to a high level (for example, you could write programs in the spreadsheet to calculate numbers) or be able to use a range of other programs like PowerPoint, Access, or specialist software related to the business such as accounts, payroll, or design software.

How Do I Know Whether the Company Is Asking About Competencies or Selection Criteria?

Sometimes employers will be obvious about the fact that they want you to address their selection criteria in your resume. You will see job advertisements with statements such as "Applicants are required to obtain the full selection criteria from the recruitment Web site at www.recruithere.com," "Selection documentation can be obtained by calling the Defense Service Center," or "Selection criteria and details on how to apply can be found on the Laughing Dog Web site, www.hadoggyha.com". In this instance, you will usually be provided with details about required resume length and any other requirements.

At other times, it is not so obvious. If an advertisement uses the heading "Requirements" and there are more than six points in total, you should create a separate attachment to address the selection criteria.

Decoding the Jargon—Qualifiers

Here are some qualifiers commonly seen in selection criteria:

- **Outstanding, superior, excellent, strong, sound:** These are the normal hyperbolic words that we have come to know and love! Do not be intimidated by them. It means they want someone who is reasonably good at something. For instance, the fact that you have the capacity for thought, language, and creativity (sometimes at the same time) sets you apart from Jim's Welsh Springer Spaniels, and therefore you possess superior, outstanding, excellent, strong, and sound skills! Note that these statements rarely state against what standard they are making the judgments of excellence, superiority, and so on. Do not be intimidated to use such positive descriptors to describe your own talents.

- **Knowledge of, understanding of:** At the very least, you've got to demonstrate that you know what they are talking about! So you might address "knowledge of wireless networking" by mentioning the names of network programs you have used, or the names of network hardware.

  You might be able to get away with "I have knowledge of wireless networking appropriate to the requirements of this position" if you are really desperate and have only slight knowledge, but are confident you could learn about this area. Remember that whatever you claim may be more closely examined in an interview, so be honest and make sure you are not stretching the truth.

  Demonstrate your knowledge with evidence wherever you can. Your reply might be "I have knowledge of wireless networks, having installed an IEEE 802.11b-compliant PCMCIA Type-II 11Mbps wireless LAN adapter in my current job."

- **Demonstrated, ability to:** This means that you are actually required to give evidence in your statements that you have done this. For instance, "demonstrated ability to exercise taste and judgment in editing the company newsletter" could be addressed with "As editor of the Departmental Circular, I had to make the decision to remove a humorous article submitted by a junior employee. The article had the capacity to offend those who did not get the joke; and because the primary goal of the publication was to inform and assist, as opposed to entertain, I was able to convince my colleague to resubmit his article with the jokes removed. I was praised on the quality of the publication under my editorship and received no complaints from the readership."
- **Background in, experience with:** This means the company is looking for evidence that you have done the tasks or competency in the past, preferably in your current or previous jobs. Generally this refers to work you've done, more than training you've completed. So emphasize work experience first and foremost, but do not omit relevant training if space permits.
- **Appreciation of:** This usually means that you've heard of the discipline or concept the advertisement is asking about, or there is a possibility that the position will have some relation to it. This wording normally does not signify the central or crucial knowledge, skills, and abilities in the job. Often it is used in relation to policies such as Equal Employment Opportunity. You do not have to be an expert in employment policies, but you do need to appreciate that the company has one and understand in broad terms what it means.

Steps in Addressing Selection Criteria

Follow these steps to create a document that addresses specific selection criteria:

1. Create a document that is separate from your resume.
2. Title this document "Statements addressing the selection criteria" (or use the phrase the employer uses in the advertisement).
3. Use each of the selection criteria as headings.
4. Address each criterion carefully, providing evidence to back up your claims.
5. Ensure that you have addressed all aspects of each selection criterion.
6. Draw upon different evidence and examples in support of different criteria. Do not repeat the same achievements over and over for each criterion.
7. Use positive and unequivocal language. Avoid using qualifiers such as "quite good," "some," "a little," "reasonable," or "average."
8. Use your job detective skills to ensure that you understand what each of the criteria means (see Chapter 3).

9. Check for a word limit (some employers stipulate the total number of pages allowable for the selection criteria). If there is no word limit indicated, you can assume it is fine to write about half a page worth of text per criterion. That's right! One or two sentences are generally not going to be sufficient. On the other hand, given that there are generally five or more statements to address, if you write much more than half a page, you run the risk of boring the reader and hence not being selected for an interview.

10. Make sure every claim you make in addressing these statements is consistent with any claims, achievements, or job history contained in your resume.

How Does This Affect the Style and Content of My Resume?

Some employers may ask you to address the selection criteria in a separate document and also to send in a resume. Now the issue arises of what to include in the resume and what to include in the selection criteria. The answer to this dilemma is that you must always fully address the selection criteria in the explicit statement headed "Addressing the selection criteria." However, that does not mean you should slack off on the resume, or that you need not include competency statements in your resume.

Clearly, you will deal with many of the competencies that you would normally have included in the resume while addressing the selection criteria. However, there may well be some that have not been included in the selection criteria that you could include to good effect in your resume—for instance, attention to detail, tenacity, and numeracy to name a few. Including additional competency statements—even if they are not requested—impresses employers. Evidence that Jim Bright published in an international selection journal with Sonia Manser shows that resumes that included extra competency statements over and above the required ones were rated even more highly than resumes that exactly addressed the competency statements and no more.

> **Note:** Do not include additional statements on your separate document entitled "Addressing the selection criteria"—this document must address exactly what you are being asked for.

If all of your competencies are fully covered in the separate document, it is still worth considering including highly abridged (succinct) statements on three or four of your most relevant other competencies. However, keep these to no more than one or two bullets or sentences. This will allow your resume to stand alone from the selection criteria document, but will not make your application package overly repetitious.

Sometimes the candidate is asked to address the selection criteria in the cover letter. Do not fall into the trap that many do of providing overly succinct, breezy, or casual statements in the belief that the cover letter needs to be short (one page). Normally you would be correct to keep the cover letter short, but in this case you have been invited to write a much longer one.

We recommend that the first page of the letter follow the template in Chapter 13. Include a statement toward the end of the letter saying "I have included a statement explicitly addressing the job criteria. I have also included my resume for your consideration." Then attach your statements addressing the job criteria (and remember to include your resume!).

Let's look at an example from the criteria we listed earlier:

> Knowledge of OHS responsibilities and commitment to attending relevant OHS training.

Here is how you might address this criterion:

> I am an employee-elected representative of our Workplace Safety Committee at Blue Blot Inc. In this capacity I am required to have a knowledge of our Occupational Health and Safety requirements from a legislative point of view as well as recognizing that best safety practice makes good business sense. I have completed the training course "Workplace Committees" accredited by OSHA in St. Louis. This was a four-day course.
>
> I also self-initiated and completed the two-day course "Workplace First Aid Level 2." I have been called upon to provide first aid to other employees, and to ensure that any accidents that occur are appropriately recorded. One accident involving faulty printing equipment required investigation by OSHA. I assisted OSHA in its investigation by organizing interviews with the appropriate parties, providing technical information in relation to the equipment (such as maintenance records), and ensuring access to the equipment. OSHA cleared Blue Blot Inc. of any responsibility for the accident and the equipment used by us has since been recalled by the manufacturer. This was considered a good outcome for Blue Blot Inc. because the alternative may have been a complete shutdown of our business. Our OHS committee meets monthly, and I am required to regularly review our OHS policies, discuss near misses, evaluate preventative measures or solutions, and identify possible training needs and courses. In my capacity as Blue Blot Inc.'s receptionist, I am required to ensure that any onsite contractors provide evidence of having undergone relevant safety training and certification before beginning work.

Put the Work in to Get the Work

Selection criteria can be intimidating for people who have not had to write this sort of material before. Even very experienced and educated people can be reduced to nervous wrecks when confronted by these requests. Put aside plenty of time to write them. Seriously consider getting professional help. Always have a friend, partner, or colleague read and critique them. Always ask the question: "Have I provided a convincing argument that directly and clearly addresses the job criteria?"

Be prepared to write and rewrite this section. It may well influence what the recruiting panel decides to ask you about during the interview. It is tragically the case that we have sat on panels where candidates we know to be excellent are rejected out of hand because they have failed to meet the selection criteria. It is a matter of procedural fairness in some organizations, so never believe that you are so well regarded that you can afford to ignore this section.

Resume Makeovers

In this chapter you will learn
- *About the issues faced by job seekers of different ages and stages*
- *How, by following our principles, you can make dramatic improvements to your resume.*

In the following examples, some of the original resumes are poor due to layout and formatting but contain good information. Others are lacking in both format and content. These example "before" resumes are typical of the ones we receive at Bright and Associates from clients wanting professional rewrites. We think that every resume for each person and each job should be carefully crafted, so what we present is not designed to be copied slavishly. Rather, we present them to illustrate how our principles of resume writing can be applied.

This chapter contains example resumes that cover some of the key career stages and issues. The job advertisements for each resume are included too, so you can see how to address the points in the advertisement. For each career stage, we list the key points to bear in mind so that you can make sure you have addressed them when you write your own resume.

High School Graduates

It can be a challenge to stand out from the crowd as a high school graduate, as you'll have had fewer opportunities to gain the same experiences as older job seekers. Generally, we advise people to omit hobbies and interests from their resume, but we make an exception for high school graduates because this section may contain evidence of your maturity, community mindedness, team abilities, and so on. High school graduates need to focus on layout, grammar, attention to detail, and addressing the selection criteria. Do not try to claim significant experience unless you truly have it, because at this stage you are selling yourself on promise rather than on past events. Nobody will expect a high school graduate to have had years of job-relevant experience, and unless such claims are supported by convincing evidence, you run the risk of recruiters dismissing you as a liar, deluded, or hopelessly out of touch with what experience really means.

Figure 15.1 is an example of a job advertisement relevant to a high school graduate. Figure 15.2 is the "before" version of the candidate's resume. Figure 15.3 is the made-over version.

Administrative Assistant

Due to expansion, an exciting opportunity exists for a person to assist the Administration Manager in a wide variety of work such as marketing mailings, customer relations, and all other aspects of administration. Applicants must possess good communication skills with the ability to work under pressure during peak work load times. Knowledge of Word and Excel essential. Package negotiable.

Send resume to:

Human Resources Director,
American Insurance Brokers
P.O. Box 86
Cleveland, OH 44101

Figure 15.1: A job advertisement for a high school graduate.

You don't need
this label or any
label—the reader
knows it's not a
ham sandwich!

An unprofessional
and too-long
e-mail address.

Resume

Anthony Aloysious Hancock
2020 Maple Dr.
Solon, OH 44139
tony_thebadman@bdonernet.com
Telephone: (330) 777-7777

Omit irrelevant
personal details.

Use bold, caps, or
larger font instead
of underline—it
looks messy.

Single
Valid driver's license

Where are duties,
achievements?

Education
2003.   Diploma, Hutt Valley High School,
Subjects: English, mathematics, economics, computer studies, general studies, geography

Work History
Feb 2004–Dec 2005   Secretary, Interact Club, Hutt Valley High School
Feb 2004–Dec 2005   Service Assistant (part-time), Radford's Furniture Store, Parma, OH

Interests and Activities
Meeting new people, computing, public speaking, regular blood donor
Feb 2004–Dec 2005 Interact Club

I am eager to learn, hardworking, and good with computers. I have an excellent attitude.

The candidate is not selling
himself. What about personal
qualities and addressing the
selection criteria?

Figure 15.2: The "before" resume.

Anthony Hancock

2020 Maple Dr.   (330) 777-7777
Solon, OH 44139   tony@hotmail.com

Career Objective

A busy, entry-level position in administration that uses my computing and organizational skills while enabling me to learn about a business from the ground up.

Skills, Experience, and Personal Attributes

Communications Skills
Developed public speaking skills while competing in Toastmasters public speaking competitions. This experience has given me the confidence to express myself clearly and confidently. As a finalist in the Toastmasters public speaking competition, was invited to present to 200 people. Regularly use written communications skills in composing correspondence and promotional material for the Interact Club.

Customer-Relations Skills
While at Radford's Furniture Store, earned "Employee of the Month" award five times. Take time to listen to customers, identify their needs, and then recommend products that are most suitable. During employment at Radford's, attended a two-day training course on customer service skills.

Time-Management Skills
While completing high school diploma, held a part-time position at Radford's as well as a serving as secretary of the Interact Club. Carefully planned school work around these extracurricular activities, never missing a school deadline or needing an extension to complete work. Schedule and complete tasks in order of priority, developing time-management skills that transfer well to the workplace.

Computer Skills
Completed a course in computer studies, including Excel, Word for Windows, Access, and PowerPoint. Ranked second in class for computer studies and highly proficient in use of these packages. As an avid computer user at home, also familiar with Internet software.

Education

Diploma, 2005, Hutt Valley High School
Subjects: English, mathematics, economics, computer studies, general studies, geography

Academic Achievements
Ranked top student in economics at Hutt Valley High School, 2005
Toastmasters Public Speaking Competition Finalist, 2005

Other Courses
Customer Service Skills, 2004 (in-house training at Radford's Furniture Store)

Figure 15.3: The "after" resume.

Anthony Hancock   Page 2
(330) 777-7777   tony@hotmail.com

Employment History

Secretary, Interact Club, Hutt Valley High School   *Feb 2004–Dec 2005*

Duties included
- Taking and typing minutes of weekly meetings.
- Composing and typing outgoing correspondence.
- Organizing mailings to students on club activities.
- Responding to incoming correspondence.

Achievements:
- Won school award for community involvement.
- Initiated mailings that increased membership from 10 to 17 members.
- Responded to all incoming mail within 7 days of receipt.

Service Assistant (Part-Time), Radford's Furniture Store, Parma, OH   *Feb 2004–Dec 2005*

Duties included
- Helping customers with location of products; explaining different features of products to customers.
- Dealing with customer complaints when products were returned.
- Serving customers at cash registers and stocking shelves with products.

Achievements:
- "Employee of the month" May 2004, Nov 2004, Feb 2005, July 2005, and September 2005 (based on customer nomination)
- Awarded employee with "Best Knowledge—Bathroom Fittings" by Caroma (supplier).

Interests and Activities

Meeting new people, computing, public speaking, regular blood donor
Interact Club, Feb 2004–Dec 2005

The After resume is much more accomplished. It is laid out well and space is not wasted on silly column structures. The key competencies clearly address the selection criteria mentioned in the job advertisement. The resume emphasizes achievements all the way through. Jobs and education are clearly explained, highlighting what was achieved.

High School Graduate Checklist

The following checklist is a quick reminder of all the key things you need for your resume:

- Name, full address, telephone numbers, up-to-date e-mail address that reflects the image you want to portray
- Full details of all paid jobs you have held
- Details of any voluntary work you may have done
- Full educational qualifications
- Details of any interests or hobbies
- Emphasis on achievements and results
- Believable competency statements backed up with evidence
- A snappy career statement
- Printed on high-quality paper

College Graduates

College graduates have several challenges. Firstly, if you have not worked while in college, you face similar issues to the high school graduate, and it might be worth checking out the preceding section. Graduates can make a couple of basic mistakes. They can be too hard on themselves; and they can lack the confidence to emphasize their knowledge, skills, abilities, and attitude. A university education, if well done, should give the graduate a realization of just how much they don't know! This can be reflected in their career thinking, which is unfortunate.

Of course, the other extreme is Mr. Know-It-All. This type of person truly believes that their degree confers upon them superhuman status and that it will do all the talking. Recruiters hate these types, and they tend to crash back to earth with a bump. Employers are increasingly interested in well-rounded applicants, and while high academic achievement is clearly desirable, they will be looking for evidence that you have made the most of all the opportunities afforded you in college. So getting involved in clubs and societies, or giving something back to the community through voluntary or charitable work, will be well received.

Leadership skills, teamwork, presentation skills, and so on, can all be gained by getting involved in extracurricular activities. These demonstrate to an employer that you are well-rounded as a person and have taken a strategic approach to getting the right competencies.

Figure 15.4 is a job advertisement directed at new college graduates. Figures 15.5 and 15.6 are the "before" and "after" versions of the resume written in response to this ad.

GRADUATE ENGINEER

ASM Power is setting a dynamic pace in the standby power market. Our current Operations and Engineering Managers joined as graduates, and their rapid progression creates openings for new graduates. A rare structured two-year development program will prepare you to master a broad engineering/operations/ management role. Commitment and enthusiasm will be required as you become involved in Production/Capacity Planning, Purchasing, Customer Liaison, Personnel Management, Process Re-Engineering, and Supplier Negotiations. You will need confident speaking and presentation skills, high computer literacy, and a willingness to embrace new ideas. Above all, you will recognize a great opportunity.

Send applications by 5 June to: David Bradshaw, HR Director, ASM Power, P.O. BOX 321, Tell City, IN 47586; bradshaw@asm.com.

Figure 15.4: A job advertisement for a new college graduate.

Avoid putting "in confidence" or confidential—is it so secret that they shouldn't read it?

Don't put full name—a waste of time and a source of mirth.

E-mail that doesn't match the name on the resume.

In confidence
Name: Hattie Joyce Grenfell Jacques
Address: 11 Ridgley St., Newburgh, IN 47630
hillK@techno.com
Telephone: (812) 465-2152

This is not the place to put computer skills. Gives no indication of how adept the candidate is with each package.

I am an avid computer user:
CAD
MS Excel
MS Word
MS Project
MS PowerPoint
WordPerfect
Netscape Navigator
Eudora Light

Bad layout, wastes a lot of page "real estate."

Education
2003   Bachelor of Science, Electrical Engineering, *cum laude*
            University of Evansville
                    Honors Thesis: "Power: It's a Passion"

Secondary
1999   Diploma
                    Harrison High School

Academic achievements
2003   University Award in Electrical Engineering
2003   Publication in *Engineering* magazine entitled "The Power or
            the Passion:
                    Energy Sources for the Future"
1999 Toastmasters public speaking finalist
Topic: "Energy Yesterday, Today, Tomorrow"

Ragged and poor formatting, especially the small bullets and the second line of each bullet—learn how to use a word processor, or find someone who knows how to use one!

Employment history
Nov 2003–Feb 2004 Associate Electrical Engineer
Summer Internship, Dockley Power Station, Boonville, IN

No reference to achievements, just a list of duties performed. It looks like a lot of "helping out."

Responsibilities
• assist electrical engineer in the design and layout of electrical installations and circuitry
• collect information, perform complex calculations, and prepare diagrams and drawings
of electrical installations and circuitry
• use CAD to produce designs and detailed drawings
• assist in testing and commissioning of electrical equipment and installations, and in
the supervision of operations and maintenance.

Interests and activities
University debating team, computer simulations, personal computing, cooking, hockey. Thesis
topic, "Power: It's a Passion," looked at applications of current technology to the generation of
power in the future. Regularly undertake own research via the Internet and numerous trade
journals to determine industry trends and identify applications to own work environment.

Complete failure to address the key job requirements as mentioned in the ad.

Figure 15.5: The "before" resume.

Hattie Jacques

11 Ridgley St.   (812) 465-2152
Newburgh, IN 47630   hattie.jacques@techno.com

Career Objective

To launch a career in electrical engineering within the power industry to further develop and use my high levels of computer literacy and confident presentation skills. The organization I am seeking is progressive and able to provide a comprehensive and structured learning program, such as offered by ASM Power.

Skills, Experience, and Personal Attributes

Speaking and Presentation Skills
Confident and articulate public speaker. Finalist at the National University debating challenge, 2004. Have presented to challenging academic panels on university honors thesis. At Dockley Power Station, was required to present my findings from the testing and evaluation of a new type of pump under consideration by management. Following my evaluation and subsequent presentation, management at Dockley Power Station went ahead with the purchase.

High Computer Literacy
Regularly use the following software:
- CAD
- MS Excel
- MS Word
- MS Project
- MS PowerPoint
- WordPerfect
- Netscape Navigator

Willingness to Embrace New Ideas
Thesis topic, "Power: It's a Passion," looked at applications of current technology to the generation of power in the future. Asked by industry journal *Engineering* to write an article on the topic, with the editorial suggesting that some of the ideas were "at the forefront of thinking around the topic." Regularly undertake own research via the Internet and numerous trade journals to determine industry trends and identify applications to own work environment.

Education

Bachelor of Science in Electrical Engineering, 2003, University of Evansville
cum laude; honors thesis: "Power: It's a Passion"

Academic Achievements
- University Award in Electrical Engineering, 2003
- 2003 Publication in *Engineering* magazine entitled "The Power or The Passion: Energy Sources for the Future," 2003
- Toastmasters public speaking finalist, 1999; Topic: "Energy Yesterday, Today, Tomorrow"

Employment History

Associate Electrical Engineer   Nov 2003–Feb 2004
Intern, Dockley Power Station, Boonville, IN

Responsibilities:
- Assisted electrical engineer in the design and layout of electrical installations and circuitry.
- Collected information, performed complex calculations, and prepared diagrams and drawings of electrical installations and circuitry.
- Used CAD to produce designs and detailed drawings.
- Assisted in testing and commissioning of electrical equipment and installations, and in the supervision of operations and maintenance.

Achievements:
- Completed new drawings for Dockley Power Station No. 1.
- Redesigned pump and outlined installation program.

Figure 15.6: The "after" resume.

This resume sets out all of the information in a much more logical manner. The selection criteria are explicitly addressed. Redundant information such as "in confidence" and "name:" are removed. Achievements are highlighted, and the layout is significantly improved.

College Graduate Checklist

The following checklist is a quick reminder of all the key things you need for your resume:

- Name, full address, telephone numbers, up-to-date e-mail address (that reflects the image you want to portray)
- Full details of all paid jobs you have held
- Details of any voluntary work you may have done
- Full educational qualifications
- Details of any interests or hobbies
- Emphasis on achievements and results
- Believable competency statements backed up with evidence
- A snappy career statement
- Printed on high-quality paper

Early Career

Early-career job hunters are looking to gain further experience and promotion. They want to maximize their limited experience and develop the necessary skills for the next step, or a broader portfolio of skills to make themselves more employable.

The challenges here include demonstrating that you are a more experienced candidate than graduate applicants. You need to make your recent job experience count so that potential employers can see that you will "hit the ground running" in the new position, and that you will not need a lot of hand-holding and basic training. Employers need to understand not just what you have previously done, but what you are capable of in the future.

Figure 15.7 is a job advertisement that may be directed at early-career candidates. Figures 15.8 and 15.9 are the "before" and "after" versions of the resume written in response to this ad.

Training Manager

Nerck Pharmaceuticals

Would you like to join the world's third biggest pharmaceutical company, currently expanding rapidly in the Midwest U.S. market? We require a manager to join our training division, where you would be responsible for the delivery of training programs to our sales staff. A dynamic, results-focused team player, you will have excellent communications skills, and will be able to handle pressure and work to deadlines. With several years of solid experience in an international company, you will be accredited in NLP and will have a basic understanding of training evaluation techniques. Reporting to our Regional Manager, you will be required to provide input into the marketing strategies for the Midwest region by training our sales staff to improve market share.

Please forward your resume to: Jim Price, Personnel Dept., Nerck Pharmaceuticals, 5800 Washington Street, Evansville, IN 47715; or jprice@nerck.com.

EOE/AA

Figure 15.7: A job ad for an early-career candidate.

Use name only; otherwise you will appear pompous.

This candidate will go to the bottom of the list with a bullet. Overuse of bullets leads to a long and messy document that looks like a computer printout—use bullet points judiciously.

Personal Details of Ms Josie Lee:

Josie Lee
- 15 Browns Rd.
- Macomb, IL 61455
- Telephone: (618) 555-5555
- Fax number: (618) 444-4444
- e-mail: Josie@comten.com

Career objective
- To build a career with a progressive learning organization that genuinely values the contribution that training can make to achieving business objectives.

Do not underline.

Skills, experience and personal attributes
- Business acumen
  - At Fish Fingers Inc., analyze business reports (sales, production) and identify training opportunities.
  - By reviewing sales figures and talking to representatives, I discovered that many were having trouble overcoming sales objections.
  - Training was designed to address this problem and sales increased by 25% two months after training.
  - Practical experience is supplemented by graduate management degree from the University of Evansville.
- Knowledge of training techniques
  - In addition to a degree in adult education, accredited NLP trainer (Level IV) who has conducted evaluations on all training courses conducted to date.
  - As a member of the Illinois Institute of Management, undertake professional development to continually update knowledge.
  - Maximize use of the best available training techniques.
- Ability to motivate others
  - At FF Inc., training courses often need to be run after hours or on weekends, cutting into sales representatives' personal lives.
  - It is important from participants' perspectives that the courses are considered worthwhile, help them to deliver results on the job, and are fun.
  - To ensure that the trainees' needs were met, on appointment at FF Inc., interviewed a cross-section of representatives, identified their needs, and designed training courses to address these.
  - Evaluations have proven these to be very successful, with participant and manager satisfaction ratings of 4 and above for 85% of courses.

Waste of page real estate.

Education
- Postsecondary
  - BA, 1998 (Adult Education)
    - Southern Illinois University, Carbondale
  - MBA, Management, 2001
    - University of Evansville
- Short Courses
  - NLP (Level IV) accreditation
    - Training for Success
  - New techniques in course evaluation
    - Illinois Institute of Management
  - Games Trainers Play
    - Training Mind-Gym, Inc.

Figure 15.8: The "before" resume.

<u>Academic achievements</u>
- Best Trainer (as evaluated by practicum trainees)
  - Awarded by the IIM

<u>Employment history</u>
- Feb 2001–current   Training Manager, Fish Fingers Inc., Macomb, IL

<u>Responsibilities</u>
- identify training needs based on business objectives.
- prepare business training plan.
- design NLP-based training courses.
- conduct training courses.
- evaluate and report on learning outcomes.
- manage training budget and expenditure.
- manage department of three staff.

<u>Achievements</u>
- 80% of courses conducted out of core business hours to minimize selling downtime
- in-house designed sales training course contributed to 25% increase in sales
- participant and manager satisfaction ratings of 4 and above for 85% of courses
- training budget on target ($150,000) and expenditure on external consultants reduced by 18%.

- Jan 1999–Jan 2000   Training Officer, Bakers Dozen, Macomb, IL

<u>Responsibilities</u>
- evaluate off-the-shelf training courses and other training resources (for example, videos)
- conduct off-the-shelf training courses
- prepare training materials
- report on training activity
- gather information on training needs
- evaluate in-house courses
- maintain training records.

Bullets give impression of more responsibilities than achievements.

<u>Achievements</u>
- implemented structured induction training courses for all new employees
- conducted courses according to training manager's training plan (on time and on budget)
- implemented new computerized training recordkeeping system.

- Jan 1995–Dec 1998   Crew Member, McDonalds, Macomb, IL

Pretty good content; shame about the layout. Could do better.

Josie Lee

15 Browns Rd., Macomb, IL 61455   (618) 555-5555 (home)
josie@comcast.net   Fax: (618) 444-4444

Career Objective

To build a career with a progressive learning organization that genuinely values the contribution that training can make to achieving business objectives.

Skills, Experience, and Personal Attributes

Business Acumen
In current position at Fish Fingers Inc., required to analyze business reports (for example, sales and production) and identify training opportunities. By reviewing sales figures and talking to representatives, discovered that many were having trouble overcoming sales rejections. Training was designed to address this problem and sales increased by 25 percent two months after training. Practical experience supplemented by and MBA from the University of Evansville.

Knowledge of Training Techniques
In addition to B.A. in adult education, accredited NLP trainer (Level IV) who has conducted evaluations on all training courses conducted to date. As a member of the Illinois Institute of Management, undertake professional development to continually update knowledge, maximizing use of the best available training techniques.

Ability to Motivate Others
At FF Inc., training courses often need to be run after hours or on weekends, cutting into sales representatives' personal lives. It is important from participants' perspectives that the courses are considered worthwhile, help them to deliver results on the job, and are fun. To ensure that the trainees' needs were met, on appointment at FF Inc. interviewed a cross-section of representatives, identified their needs, and designed training courses to address these. Evaluations have proven these courses to be very successful, with participant and manager satisfaction ratings of 4 and above for 85 percent of courses.

Education

MBA, Management, 2001, University of Evansville
B.A., Adult Education, 1998, Southern Illinois University, Carbondale

Academic Achievements
  ▪ Best Trainer, 1998 (as evaluated by practicum trainees)

Continuing Education
  ▪ NLP (Level IV) accreditation, Training for Success   2002
  ▪ New techniques in course evaluation, Illinois Institute of Management 2003
  ▪ Games Trainers Play, Training Mind-Gym, Inc.   2004

Employment History

Training Manager   Feb 2001–Present
Fish Fingers Inc., Macomb, IL

Responsibilities:
Identify training needs based on business objectives, prepare business training plan, design NLP-based training courses, conduct training courses, evaluate and report on learning outcomes, manage training budget and expenditure, and manage department of three staff.

Figure 15.9: The "after" resume.

Josie Lee   page 2
(618) 555-5555 (home)   josie@comcast.net

Achievements:
- 80 percent of courses conducted out of core business hours to minimize selling downtime.
- In-house-designed sales training course contributed to 25 percent increase in sales.
- Participant and manager satisfaction ratings of 4 and above for 85 percent of courses.
- Training budget on target ($150,000) and expenditure on external consultants reduced by 18 percent.

Training Officer   Jan 1999–Jan 2001
Bakers Dozen, Macomb, IL

Responsibilities:
Evaluate off-the-shelf training courses and other training resources (for example, videos), conduct off-the-shelf training courses, prepare training materials, report on training activity, gather information on training needs, evaluate in-house courses, and maintain training records.

Achievements:
- Implemented structured induction training courses for all new employees.
- Conducted courses according to training manager's training plan (on time and on budget).
- Implemented new computerized training recordkeeping system.

Crew Member   Jan 1995–Dec 1998
McDonalds, Macomb, IL

Early-Career Checklist

The following checklist is a quick reminder of all the key things you need for your resume:

- Name, full address, telephone numbers, up-to-date e-mail address
- Full details of all paid jobs you have held
- Details of any volunteer work you may have done
- Full educational qualifications
- Emphasis on achievements and results
- Believable competency statements backed up with evidence
- Evidence that you have moved beyond the graduate-level capability
- A snappy career statement
- Printed on high-quality paper

Mid-Career

The mid-career candidate is likely to have developed a broad portfolio of skills, as well as showing some specialization and achievement in at least one of those areas. The mid-career applicant is more likely to have a history of managing teams or groups, or a sustained history of achievement within his or her specialization. The mid-career person who is ambitious will be looking for a position that will provide a springboard to the higher echelons of the profession. Alternatively, mid-career applicants may be looking to consolidate their position or broaden their experience by moving from one industry sector (such as banking and finance) to another (such as manufacturing). Finally, mid-career applicants may be embarking on a change of career direction. Depending on how radical the change is, the mid-career-change applicant might apply for positions at an equivalent level in the new career, or they may decide to start at a relatively lower position on the new career ladder in order to get into the field.

The challenge for the mid-career applicant is to present their experience as a strong selling point, and to try to convey continued enthusiasm and passion for what it is they are doing. Employers will be on the lookout for signs of burnout or disillusionment (perhaps evidenced by a rapid succession of brief stints over the last couple of years). If you have held any positions for less than a year, be prepared to provide an explanation for this that shows you in a positive light.

Figure 15.10 is an advertisement directed to a mid-career candidate. Figures 15.11 and 15.12 are the "before" and "after" versions of the resume written in response to this ad.

Financial Accountant

This is a fixed-term contract for a modern Missouri Valley–based manufacturing site. Although supervising five people, the position is very much "hands on," which requires a willingness to take on detail and the ability to juggle multiple tasks. We seek a computer-literate accountant with experience with Microsoft systems and accounting experience, which must include tax and general ledger. You will need to be a CPA or ACA and possess strong written and verbal communication skills. Ideally, you will have manufacturing experience. However, it is unlikely that candidates with less than five years of accounting experience will have sufficient background for the position. This opportunity is available now. Please call or send details to:

Mark Matthews
Person Inc.
P.O. Box 321, Newburgh, IN 47630
Telephone (812) 555-5555 or fax (812) 444-4444
mmatthews@person.com

Figure 15.10: An ad for a mid-career candidate.

Never, ever include clip art or pictures! We see it and it never fails to get a negative reaction (perhaps it should have been a turkey?)

High Flyer

Benjamin Hill

P.O. Box 9999
Newburgh, IN 47630
  Mobile:
E-mail address:
BenjaminH@HeliInc.com

Telephone: (812) 222-2222
Fax number: (812) 333-3333
(812) 555-5555
scuttle@fred.com

Don't give a list of demands and do not give any reasons for the employer to worry about your personal life.

Career objective
I need a job near Newburgh for personal reasons. It must be with a high-quality and sympathetic employer with generous rewards for talent.

Skills, experience, and personal attributes
Accounting expertise
My computing skills include use of Word for Windows, Excel, and Access for reporting and recordkeeping.

Attention to detail
I cannot remember any instances where work has been returned to me for correction, or work has been withdrawn once errors were recognized.

Ability to manage multiple tasks
I have been required to work toward numerous and competing deadlines.

Underlining is messy, so avoid it. Also, no differentiation between headings; they are all the same size and are all equally highlighted. Use bigger and bolder designs for important headings and less emphasis for subheadings and be consistent in their use.

Education

Don't use colored backgrounds or highlights—it can look terrible when photocopied.

1990   Bachelor of Science (Accounting)
University of Evansville, Indiana

Memberships
1993   Member, American Institute of Certified Public Accountants
2002   Member, American Institute of Company Directors

Employment history
Dec 1998–Present   Financial Controller, Helicopters Inc., Boonville, IN

Responsibilities
- preparation, consolidation, and review of management and project reporting
- overseeing the preparation of progress claims and analysis and reporting on cash flow
- controlling and covering all foreign-exchange exposures
- ensuring that all insurance requirements for the project and contract are met
- liaison with banks for provision of security required under the contracts and subcontracts
- supervision of two accounting staff

Feb 1994–Nov 1998   Assistant Financial Controller, Helicopters Inc., Boonville, IN

Responsibilities
- consolidation and preparation of management and statutory accounts, tax returns, and budgets
- review and analysis of operating results for senior management
- overseeing the preparation of monthly board reports
- developing and implementing foreign-exchange trading procedures and systems
- review and support of capital expenditure proposals

Achievements
- implemented new foreign-exchange trading procedures and systems
- all reporting deadlines met

Dec 1991–Jan 1994   Tax Advisor, H&R Block, Evansville, IN

Poor layout, few achievements, no attempt to address the selection criteria, career objective counterproductive and reads like a set of demands and also hints at personal turmoil—not a good strategy!

Figure 15.11: The "before" resume.

Benjamin Hill

42 Lake View Drive
Newburgh, IN 47630
scuttle@fred.com

(812) 222-2222
Fax: (812) 333-3333
Mobile: (812) 555-5555

Career Objective

A "hands-on" senior financial role that provides challenge and capitalizes on 15 years of accounting expertise.

Skills, Experience, and Personal Attributes

Accounting Expertise
Varied finance background in both the public and private sectors. Experience at H&R Block afforded a thorough understanding of financial reporting requirements. Eleven years of experience in the controller's office at Helicopters Inc., working primarily in the areas of taxation and general ledger. Computing skills include Word, Excel, and Access for reporting and recordkeeping.

Attention to Detail
Deliver a quality reporting product that the management team can have confidence in. Outstanding record of error-free work. Rated "Highly Commendable" for attention to detail on most recent performance review.

Ability to Manage Multiple Tasks
Work toward numerous and competing deadlines. Careful planning and some delegation have resulted in successful fulfillment of all processing and reporting deadlines. Take a team approach, and manage the group's activity as well as actively participate in completing the work, resulting in the best possible outcome.

Education

Bachelor of Science, Accounting, University of Evansville, 1991

Memberships
American Institute of Certified Public Accountants
American Institute of Company Directors

Employment History

Financial Controller   Dec 1998–Present
Helicopters Inc., Boonville, IN

Responsibilities:
Prepare, consolidate, and review management and project reporting; oversee the preparation of progress claims and analysis and reporting on cash flow; control and cover all foreign-exchange exposures, ensuring that all insurance requirements for the project and contract are met; liaise with banks for provision of security required under contracts and subcontracts; supervise two accounting staff.

Achievements:
- Implemented new project reporting system to suit management team needs.
- Met all management reporting deadlines.
- Reduced time spent compiling information in department by 65 percent.
- Substituted for Vice President of Accounting in his absence.

Assistant Financial Controller   Feb 1994–Nov 1998
Helicopters Inc., Boonville, IN
Consolidated and prepared management and statutory accounts, tax returns, and budgets; reviewed and analyzed operating results for senior management; oversaw the preparation of monthly board reports; developed and implemented foreign-exchange trading procedures and systems; reviewed and supported capital expenditure proposals.

Achievements:
Implemented new foreign-exchange trading procedures and systems, with all reporting deadlines met.

Tax Adviser   Dec 1991–Jan 1994
H&R Block, Evansville, IN

Figure 15.12: The "after" resume.

This resume makeover outlines Benjamin's competencies in a more persuasive way. We have removed the clip art and the desperation from his resume. The layout looks more professional and it is easier to read.

Mid-Career Checklist

The following checklist is a quick reminder of all the key things you need for your resume:

- Name, full address, telephone numbers, up-to-date e-mail address
- Full details of all paid jobs you have held
- Details of any volunteer work you may have done
- Emphasis on achievements and results
- Believable competency statements backed up with evidence
- Evidence of sustained achievement
- Evidence of energy and enthusiasm
- A snappy career statement if you're changing careers
- Full educational qualifications
- Printed on high-quality paper

Mature Career

Candidates with a mature career are likely to have been working for perhaps 15 to 20 years, which conventionally would put them in their 40s or above. Recruiters will be looking for applicants in this pool who have demonstrated successful and extensive management skills, perhaps across a range of industry sectors. Often roles at this level will be focused on developing plans and strategies for the business. It is often the case that the technical skills that got you to this point are now less important than managerial skills, reputation, and potential managerial skills. The challenge for some will be to demonstrate that they are now ready for the move up from a technical focus to a broader, "bigger picture" focus, and also that they possess good commercial or political skills. This is not the place for the tactless blunderer or people who cannot read a profit-and-loss statement!

Figure 15.13 is a job advertisement for a mature-career candidate. Figures 15.14 and 15.15 are the "before" and "after" versions of the resume written in response to this ad.

General Manager—Technology

Our client, a national leading retailer, is seeking a General Manager to lead its business in a period of strong growth here and overseas.

The job

Principally the job will focus on developing a strategic IT plan that supports business objectives and future system requirements. There is a need to review and evaluate existing hardware/software and to manage a small support team.

The person

You are a business manager first and foremost who understands the retail industry. You have a thorough understanding of information technology, including current and future directions across the Internet/Intranet and Extranet. You possess strong people-management skills and appreciate the importance of getting the best out of your staff. You have exceptional presentation skills and can tailor content to suit a broad audience. Excellent written presentation skills are required to communicate organizational needs and persuade senior management to implement system changes. This is an excellent opportunity for a successful individual to join a rapidly developing organization and to make an impact on its future direction.

Please send your resume to:

Claudia Joy
Claudia Joy Management Recruiting, Inc.
P.O. Box 3200
Kansas City, MO 63104

Figure 15.13: An ad for a mature-career candidate.

Resume

Peter Sellars

P.O. Box 321

Kansas City, MO 63105

Telephone: (816) 555-5555 Fax number: (816) 444-4444

Mobile: (816) 664-6465

E-mail: psellars@gardener.com

The Courier font is dated and makes it look as though it was done on a typewriter.

Skills, experience and personal attributes

Leadership

As the group leader in Information Technology, identify the strategic technological and systems requirements of all retail stores. This is achieved by linking current and anticipated business needs with available technology. The Internet shopping site is a prime example of this. Leading a team of store mangers, merchandising managers, and IT managers, we identified business needs, concerns, and strategies. Under my leadership, the site was developed and launched within 18 months of conception.

Avoid this commonly recommended two-column layout—it wastes page real estate, puts too much emphasis on the headings and dates, and leaves insufficient space to lay out your achievements neatly.

Knowledge of the retail industry

Have worked in the retail industry for entire career, starting out at the bottom as a retail assistant, moving into a role as Customer Service Manager, leading an in-store IT team as the IT Manager, and finally working up to a corporate role. Unique grounding enables me to fully understand the day-to-day operations of a store as well as its management.

Business management

As Senior Manager, New Technology, required to demonstrate a sound knowledge of each store's business requirements and strategic direction. Have supplemented work experience with an MBA. Key projects that have resulted in both cost savings and efficiency improvements include fully integrated communications system and supplier, resulting in an average cost savings of half a million dollars per store; introduction of new technology to better monitor in-store trading patterns and provide links back to staffing requirements; and implementation of new POS technology without disruption to trading pattern.

Figure 15.14: The "before" resume.

Education

2003	Master of Business Administration University of Missouri, Kansas City
1996	Bachelor of Information Technology University of Missouri, Kansas City
1993	Certificate, Retail Strategic Management, Kansas City Community College

Employment history

Dec 1995—current   Senior Manager, New Technology, Raspberry Holdings, Inc., Head Office, Kansas City, MO

Duties included
- indirect responsibility for all in-store IT managers
- development of corporate IT plan
- management of corporate IT objectives
- monitoring of IT standards across stores
- identification and selection of hardware and software for stores' in-house use
- implementation of new online shopping systems
- implementation of Intranet and video technology linking store
- integration and selection of other new technology including POS, telephones, and paging
- management team on-floor communications.

Achievements
- fully integrated communications system and supplier introduced to all stores over an 18-month period with an average cost saving of half a million dollars per store
- all IT objectives outlined in 2002/3 corporate plan achieved
- introduction of weekly videoconferencing with IT in-store managers to ensure sharing of best practices and improve communication
- online shopping system introduced, returning $10 million in first week of operation with average growth of 15% per week and no loss of sales to individual stores.

It's starting to look like a list and it just keeps going on and on and on and...

Dec 1995—Nov 1999	IT Manager, Raspberry Holdings, Inc., Kansas City, MO

Duties included
- management of IT team (three staff)
- maintenance of in-store systems
- evaluation of software for store
- testing of new software for store
- implementation of new software
- implementation of backup and recovery systems.

Achievements
- identified and introduced new technology "Sales to Staffing" to better monitor in-store trading patterns and provide links back to staffing requirements
- implementation of new POS technology without disruption to trading pattern
- recovery systems worked in 100% of cases, resulting in no down time due to computer failure
- recruited and developed own replacement over a two-year period

...on and on and...

Dec 1991—Jan 1994	• Customer Service Manager, Raspberry Holdings, Inc., Kansas City, MO

- Duties included:
- staff scheduling
- performance management
- training and development
- monitoring service standards
- stock management and merchandising
- management of budgets for "Homewares"
- management and staff utilization reporting
- organizing special product promotions.

The format makes the resume look overly long and repetitious. It gives the impression that the candidate does not really know his way around word-processing software. Perhaps he even has a secretary who does his word-processing for him?

Achievements
- budgets on target 85% of the time
- sales targets achieved and exceeded 85%
- named "Customer Service Manager of the Year" by the store manager
- successful selection and promotion of two staff members to the customer service manager traineeship.

Summary of other jobs   Dec 1989—Nov 1991 Raspberry Holdings, Inc., Kansas City, MO

Not a bad resume from a content point of view, but it comes across badly with this out-of-date and difficult-to-read layout. This layout is probably the most common we see—but that's not a recommendation.

Peter Sellars

P.O. Box 321
Kansas City, MO 63105
psellars@gardener.com

(816) 555-5555
Fax: (816) 444-4444
Mobile: (816) 664-6465

Career Objective

To contribute to the successful growth and management of a retailing organization by leading initiatives to link business needs with technological solutions.

Skills, Experience, and Personal Attributes

Leadership
As the group leader in Information Technology, identify the strategic technological and systems requirements of all retail stores by linking current and anticipated business needs with available technology. The Internet shopping site is a prime example of this. Leading a team of store mangers, merchandising managers, and IT managers, we identified business needs, concerns, and strategies. Under my leadership, the site was developed and launched within 18 months of conception.

Knowledge of the Retail Industry
Have worked in the retail industry for entire career, starting out at the bottom as a retail assistant, moving into a role as Customer Service Manager, leading an in-store IT team as the IT Manager, and finally working up to a corporate role. Unique grounding enables me to fully understand the day-to-day operations of a store as well as its management.

Business Management
As Senior Manager, New Technology, required to demonstrate a sound knowledge of each store's business requirements and strategic direction. Have supplemented work experience with an MBA. Key projects that have resulted in both cost savings and efficiency improvements include fully integrated communications system and supplier, resulting in an average cost savings of half a million dollars per store; introduction of new technology to better monitor in-store trading patterns and provide links back to staffing requirements; and implementation of new POS technology without disruption to trading pattern.

Education

Master of Business Administration, 2003
Bachelor of Information Technology, 1996
Certificate, Retail Strategic Management, 1993

University of Missouri, Kansas City
University of Missouri, Kansas City
Kansas City Community College

Employment History

Senior Manager
New Technology, Raspberry Holdings, Inc., Head Office, Kansas City, MO
Dec 1999–Present

Duties included:
Indirect responsibility for all in-store IT managers; development of corporate IT plan; management of corporate IT objectives; monitoring of IT standards across stores; identification and selection of hardware and software for stores' in-house use; implementation of new online shopping systems; implementation of Intranet and video technology linking stores; and integration and selection of other new technology including POS, telephones, paging, and management team on-floor communication.

Figure 15.15: The "after" resume.

Peter Sellars   page 2
psellars@gardener.com   (816) 555-5555

Achievements:
- Fully integrated communications system and supplier introduced to all stores over an 18-month period, with an average cost saving of half a million dollars per store.
- All IT objectives outlined in 2002/03 corporate plan achieved.
- Introduction of weekly videoconferencing with IT in-store managers to ensure sharing of best practices and improve communication.
- Online shopping system introduced, returning $10 million in first week of operation with average growth of 15 percent per week and no loss of sales to individual stores.

IT Manager
Raspberry Holdings, Inc., Kansas City, MO
Dec 1995–Nov 1999

Duties included:
Management of IT team (three staff); maintenance of in-store systems; evaluation, testing, and implementation of software for store; implementation of backup and recovery systems.

Achievements:
- Identified and introduced new technology "Sales to Staffing" to better monitor in-store trading patterns and provide links back to staffing requirements.
- Implemented new POS technology without disruption to trading pattern.
- Recovery systems worked in 100 percent of all cases, resulting in no down time due to computer failure.
- Recruited and developed own replacement over a two-year period.

Customer Service Manager
Raspberry Holdings, Inc., Kansas City, MO
Dec 1991–1994

Duties included:
Management of retail service team, including staff scheduling, performance management, training, and development; monitoring service standards; stock management and merchandising; management of budgets for "Homewares"; management and staff utilization reporting; and organizing special product promotions.

Achievements:
- Budgets on target 85 percent of the time.
- Sales targets achieved and exceeded 85 percent of the time.
- Named "Customer Service Manager of the Year" by the store manager.
- Successful selection and promotion of two staff members to the customer service manager traineeship.

Summary of Other Jobs
Dec 1989–Nov 1991   Raspberry Holdings, Inc., Retail Assistant, Kansas City, MO

Mature-Career Checklist

The following checklist is a quick reminder of all the key things you need for your resume:

- Name, full address, telephone numbers, and up-to-date e-mail address
- Details of all relevant jobs you have held, omitting trivial or very low-level positions from your early career
- Details of any voluntary work you may have done if it demonstrates leadership or responsible community involvement commensurate with your executive status
- Emphasis on achievements and results
- Believable competency statements backed up with evidence
- Evidence of sustained achievement
- Evidence of energy and enthusiasm
- Evidence of abilities to step up or across into strategic management, if relevant to the position
- Full educational qualifications
- Printed on high-quality paper

Returning from a Break

Many people have a break in their careers for all sorts of reasons. Some of these reasons are

- Having a baby
- Caring for a family member
- Injury or illness
- Travel
- Relocation of a partner
- Layoff or unemployment
- Further training or education

Despite what some commentators say, our research found that employers did not look favorably on breaks in employment unless they were for full-time academic study. However, you can easily make up for this by working hard to target your resume to the job advertisement. Explain gaps briefly and quickly move on to paint a positive picture of where you see yourself going and how you can contribute to the company. Don't be tempted to dwell on negative events such as an illness. Instead, the message to get across is that the period when the gap occurred is now completely behind you and that you are ready and willing to go once more and have a significant contribution to make to this organization.

Figure 15.16 is an ad that is being targeted by a candidate with a break in his or her career. Figures 15.17 and 15.18 are the "before" and "after" versions of the resume written in response to this ad.

Computer Analyst/Programmer

An outstanding opportunity exists to join our leading-edge software consulting firm as an Analyst Programmer using the latest client/server technology. We are looking for a creative and innovative thinker who has a strong desire to be the best they can be in an environment that offers vast opportunities and rewards to dedicated and determined staff. You will be working and/or be trained alongside some of the best software developers in the field. Experience in Visual Basic, Access, SQL Server, and Internet development with tertiary qualifications is very helpful. If you are ambitious and have an enthusiastic personality, you are ideal for these challenging and exciting jobs. Top salary and compensation, bonuses and incentives, with interstate and/or international travel opportunities for the right applicant/s. We are committed to the principles of equity and diversity.

Send resume to:
Human Resources Director,
Softly Softly Inc.
P.O. Box 6654
Detroit, MI 45038

Figure 15.16: An ad targeted by a candidate who has had a break in his or her career.

Margaret Dumont
15 Fox Trot Boulevard, Detroit, MI 45000
Telephone: (313) 888-8888
Fax number: (313) 888-8889
E-mail: jenny@messages.com.au Maggie@home.com.au
Married
1 child: Demi-Teass; born May 1990; 8 lbs., 4 oz.

Irrelevant and possibly off-putting personal detail—omit.

Another appallingly self-centered career objective—avoid jokes, sarcasm, and personal detail.

Career Objective
To get back some sanity and adult company after the birth of my daughter Demi-Teass Dumont and subsequent career break. To use the skills I learned the hard way in college retraining. To get my previously successful career back on track.

Focus on how you can replicate your success, not how long ago it was.

Ability to Develop New Products
Some time ago I previously wrote two award-winning and innovative software packages ("Ms. Terry Investigates" and "Y? Y? Y?"), with sales of the latter package exceeding budget expectations by 150% ($2.3 million). During my college career, I wrote two additional products judged by Human Side to be the best software products available of their kind. My degree has provided me with up-to-date knowledge in Visual Basic, Access, SQL Server, and Internet technology.

Ambitious
With several years of experience in programming and product development, I am now eager to fulfill my ultimate potential in a demanding and challenging role at Softly, Softly, Inc. While at Educational Software, Inc., I was promoted from programmer to senior programmer within two years based on my performance. When I relocated with my partner to Pasadena, I took the opportunity to pursue relevant studies so that the up-to-date knowledge would help me achieve my future career goals.

Knowledge of Client/Server Technology
I led a project team exploring the application of client/server technology to a large telecommunications company. Using C/ST, we were able to help the client introduce a complex customer billing system that was simple and more cost-effective. I am familiar with many of the client/servers and their capabilities through my own Internet research.

This makes the employer think, "Will she pack up and leave again?" Just focus on developing knowledge that contributes to career goals.

Education
2002	Bachelor of Information Technology University of Michigan	
1992	Certificate in Information Technology Detroit Community College	

Academic Achievements
2002	Best university software product Awarded by Human Side
2001	Best university educational software product Awarded by Human Side

Employment History
Feb 1994–Dec 1995   Senior Programmer, Educational Software, Detroit, MI

Responsibilities
- same as for "Programmer" (see below), with additional responsibility for the supervision, development, and performance management of eight software programmers

Achievements
- team responsible for seven award-winning packages during the period I was supervising
- sales of educational packages increased by 80% during the period I was supervising

Figure 15.17: The "before" resume.

With this type of formatting, it's easy
to get lost in the detail.

Feb 1992–Jan 1994   Programmer, Educational Software, Detroit, MI
Responsibilities
- document computer user's requirements with analysts
- analyze objectives and software requirements identified by analysts
- write programs for educational software
- prepare support documentation for computer users and support personnel
- test and evaluate programs prepared by other programmers

Achievements
- wrote "Ms. Terry Investigates," winner of the 1995 educational software package of the year
- sales of educational package "Y? Y? Y?" exceeded budget expectations by 150% ($2.3 million)

Jan 1990–Jan 1992   PC Support Officer, Legal Eagles Inc., Detroit, MI
Responsibilities
- software and hardware selection
- testing software prior to installation
- systems planning
- installation of software and hardware systems
- maintenance of systems
- basic programming

Achievements
- installation of major software upgrade (150 users) without loss of business time
- selection of software package that saved $50K in business operating expenses

Interests and activities
New Internet products, interactive computer games

Margaret Dumont

15 Fox Trot Boulevard
Detroit, MI 45000

(313) 888-8888
Fax: (313) 888-8889
mdumont@work.com

Career Objective

To achieve my ultimate potential in an innovative and commercial environment that fully utilizes my IT qualifications, experience, and creativity.

Skills, Experience, and Personal Attributes

Ability to Develop New Products
Wrote award-winning and innovative software packages ("Ms. Terry Investigates" and "Y? Y? Y?"), with sales of the latter exceeding budget expectations by 150 percent ($2.3 million). While earning college degree, wrote two additional products judged by Human Side to be the best software products of their kind available. Up-to-date knowledge in Visual Basic, Access, SQL Server, and Internet technology.

Ambition
Several years of experience in programming and product development. While at Educational Software Inc., promoted from the role of programmer to senior programmer within two years based on excellent performance. Pursued relevant college studies, earning up-to-date knowledge that will help me to achieve my future career goals.

Knowledge of Client/Server Technology
Led a project team exploring the application of client/server technology to a large telecommunications company. Using C/ST, helped the client introduce a complex customer billing system that was simple and more cost-effective. Familiar with many of the client/servers and their capabilities through own Internet research.

Education

Bachelor of Information Technology	2002
University of Michigan	
Certificate in Information Technology	1992
Detroit Community College	

Academic Achievements

Best University Software Product	2002
Awarded by Human Side	
Best University Educational Software Product	2001
Awarded by Human Side	

Employment History

Senior Programmer   Educational Software, Detroit, MI
Feb 1994–Dec 1995

Responsibilities
Same as "Programmer" (see below), with additional responsibility for the supervision, development, and performance management of eight software programmers.

Achievements
- Team responsible for seven award-winning packages under my supervision.
- Sales of educational packages increased by 80 percent under my direction.

Figure 15.18: The "after" resume.

Margaret Dumont

15 Fox Trot Boulevard
Detroit, MI 45000

(313) 888-8888
Fax: (313) 888-8889
mdumont@work.com

Career Objective

To achieve my ultimate potential in an innovative and commercial environment that fully utilizes my IT qualifications, experience, and creativity.

Skills, Experience, and Personal Attributes

Ability to Develop New Products
Wrote award-winning and innovative software packages ("Ms. Terry Investigates" and "Y? Y? Y?"), with sales of the latter exceeding budget expectations by 150 percent ($2.3 million). While earning college degree, wrote two additional products judged by Human Side to be the best software products of their kind available. Up-to-date knowledge in Visual Basic, Access, SQL Server, and Internet technology.

Ambition
Several years of experience in programming and product development. While at Educational Software Inc., promoted from the role of programmer to senior programmer within two years based on excellent performance. Pursued relevant college studies, earning up-to-date knowledge that will help me to achieve my future career goals.

Knowledge of Client/Server Technology
Led a project team exploring the application of client/server technology to a large telecommunications company. Using C/ST, helped the client introduce a complex customer billing system that was simple and more cost-effective. Familiar with many of the client/servers and their capabilities through own Internet research.

Education

Bachelor of Information Technology	2002
University of Michigan	
Certificate in Information Technology	1992
Detroit Community College	

Academic Achievements

Best University Software Product	2002
Awarded by Human Side	
Best University Educational Software Product	2001
Awarded by Human Side	

Employment History

Senior Programmer
Feb 1994–Dec 1995

Educational Software, Detroit, MI

Responsibilities
Same as "Programmer" (see below), with additional responsibility for the supervision, development, and performance management of eight software programmers.

Achievements
- Team responsible for seven award-winning packages under my supervision.
- Sales of educational packages increased by 80 percent under my direction.

Returning from a Break Checklist

The following checklist is a quick reminder of all the key things you need for your resume:

- Name, full address, telephone numbers, and up-to-date e-mail address
- Full details of all paid jobs you have held
- Details of any voluntary work you may have done
- Emphasis on achievements and results
- Believable competency statements backed up with evidence
- Not dwelling on the gaps
- Evidence of energy and enthusiasm
- A snappy career statement focusing on future contributions you can make
- Full educational qualifications
- Printed on high-quality paper

Career Change

Two catch-phrases in the human resources area are "transferable skills" and "transfer of training." All they mean is taking something you learned in one place and using it successfully in another. If you have ever played golf, you might have practiced for hours on the driving range to perfect your swing, but the real test comes when you are out on the course in a match tournament. Some groups of people have skills that overlap a lot, so it is not uncommon for baseball players to be good golfers, and there are lots of lawyers who end up in amateur or professional acting roles. For baseball players, batting and hitting a golf ball require broadly similar skills. For the lawyers, if you can get up and think on your feet in front of a judge and jury, performing in front of an audience is a piece of cake!

The challenge for the career changer is to look into their past working life and pull out all the knowledge, skills, abilities, and attitudes that may enable him or her to make a contribution to the new career. The career changer has to reshape their past working lives to show their accumulated experience in a new light that maximizes the similarity between them and the job.

Figure 15.19 is an ad targeted by a career changer. Figures 15.20 and 15.21 are the "before" and "after" versions of the resume written in response to this ad.

Sales Representatives

Deci Co. in Orlando requires Sales Representatives to expand their sales to corporate clients. While experience in the printing industry is not essential, a proven sales and service ability in the above market would be a clear advantage. You should be highly motivated and focused on building a client base. You understand that success comes from building relationships with customers and tenaciously developing and promoting printing solutions to a wide industry client base. This position suits a practical results-driven achiever who seeks an attractive compensation package.

Please send resume to:
Douglas Giles
Giles Recruitment
P.O. Box 22679
Orlando, FL 32876

Figure 15.19: An ad targeted by a career changer.

Avoid the "confidential" pomposity
and do not use silly fonts.

CONFIDENTIAL RESUME OF:

Terrance Thomas
P.O. Box 321
Orlando, FL 32879
Mobile:

Telephone: (407) 888-8888
Fax number: (407) 888-8889
(407) 888-8887   E-mail: terry@hotmail.com

Humor or nega-
tive self-appraisal
is a bad idea—
this gives a poor
impression.

Career Objective

Tired, disillusioned, and plateaued. You will provide me with the challenge to once again find
enjoyment at work.

Employment History

Jul 1997–May 2005   Purchasing Manager, Night Eye Cameras, Inc., Orlando, FL
Responsibilities
identify new opportunities and develop strategies to achieve business objectives
develop and improve vendor relations
implement procurement systems to maximize profit
vendor management of contracts in excess of $12 million

Inconsistent format-
ting suggests that
there is a single job
listed rather than
two separate jobs.

Oct 1994–Jul 1997   Distribution Officer, Night Eye Cameras Inc., Orlando, FL
Responsibilities
- rationalize distribution strategy
- develop methods to reduce product transit damage
- manage the inventory of product for under warranty/repair
- control international and national freight accounts
- coordinate dispatches to customers and sales offices worldwide

Jun 1993–May 1994   Records Management, Sony Music, Miami, FL
Apr 1990–April 1993   Logistics/ Supply Officer, U.S. Navy

Detailing where the
course was conducted
helps people evaluate its
worth. You would never
guess that two of these
courses were from an
industry association.

Education

2003   A.S., Business (Marketing)
          University of Florida
Continuing Education
1995   Purchasing Contract Negotiation
                        American Institute of Purchasing Professionals
1998   Purchasing and Inventory Control Systems and Supply
Management
                        American Institute of Purchasing Professionals

Irrelevant to job—
fishing/computing
possibly imply the
candidate is a "loner,"
which is not a good
quality for a sales job.

Interests and Activities

Rugby league, fishing, golf, personal computing

Figure 15.20: The "before" resume.

Terrance Thomas

P.O. Box 321
Orlando, FL 32879
terry@hotmail.com

Home: (407) 888-8888
Fax: (407) 888-8889
Mobile: (407) 888-8887

Career Objective

To use my selling and customer service skills in a representative role that focuses on building relationships with existing customers, as well as translating opportunities into new accounts.

Skills, Experience, and Personal Attributes

Selling Skills
Identifying new opportunities and developing strategies to turn these into reality. In purchasing positions, have developed a unique insight into your customers' needs from their perspective. Understand the importance of their needs being identified, turning your product features into customer benefits, and closing a deal that benefits both supplier and customer.

Customer Service
By developing better relationships with vendors and suppliers, generate significant improvements to customer service at Night Eye Cameras, Inc. Introduced a system to support the introduction of new products, including better documentation, customer training, and a customer hot line to deal with product queries quickly. The key to good customer service is servicing existing clients as if you were trying to win their business for the first time. It is important to understand what is most important to them and then to address this need.

Motivation
Achieved significant cost savings and efficiency improvements in previous positions and look forward to the opportunity to do the same thing for Deci Co. Establish professional and personal goals for myself and then work to achieve these as quickly as possible. These efforts have been recognized and rewarded in the form of promotions.

Employment History

Purchasing Manager   Jul 1997–May 2005
Night Eye Cameras, Inc., Orlando, FL

Responsibilities
Identify new opportunities and develop strategies to achieve business objectives, develop and improve vendor relations, implement procurement systems to maximize profit, and manage vendor contracts in excess of $12 million.

Achievements
- Saved six-digit sums in material expenditure annually.
- Successfully negotiated supply contracts with more than ten offshore vendors.
- Implemented cost-reduction techniques to make California-based manufacturing more cost-effective than east coast contract assemblers.
- Implemented a successful vendor assistance program targeting new product support.
- Optimized storage facilities with the adoption of improved stock-handling methods.

Figure 15.21: The "after" resume.

Terrance Thomas
terry@hotmail.com

Distribution Officer   Oct 1994–Jul 1997
Night Eye Cameras, Inc., Orlando, FL

Responsibilities
Rationalized distribution strategy, developed methods to reduce product transit damage, managed the inventory of product under warranty/repair, controlled international and national freight accounts, and coordinated dispatches to customers and sales offices worldwide.

Achievements
- Consolidated freight services, resulting in an increase of corporate bargaining power.
- Reduced transit damage to under 0.5 percent.

Jun 1993–May 1994   Records Management, Sony Music, Miami, FL
Apr 1990–April 1992   Logistics/ Supply Officer, U.S. Navy

Education

A.S. in Business (Marketing), 2003
University of Florida

Purchasing Contract Negotiation, American Institute of Purchasing Professionals, 1995

Purchasing and Inventory Control Systems and Supply Management, American Institute of Purchasing Professionals, 1998

Career Change Checklist

The following checklist is a quick reminder of all the key things you need for your resume:

- Name, full address, telephone numbers, and up-to-date e-mail address
- Full details of all paid jobs you have held, emphasizing those most relevant to the new career
- Details of any voluntary work you may have done
- Emphasis on achievements and results
- Believable competency statements backed up with evidence linking your old career competencies to the new required competencies
- Evidence of sustained achievement
- Evidence of energy and enthusiasm
- A snappy career statement
- Full educational qualifications
- Printed on high-quality paper

Tricky Resume Issues

In this chapter, you will learn more about
- *Dealing with potential prejudice on the part of employers*
- *Dealing with gaps in your employment history*
- *Electronic resumes*
- *The steps in the recruitment process*
- *Including references on your resume*
- *Including a photograph on your resume*

Dealing with Prejudice

One of the most commonly asked questions about writing a resume is what to do about bias. This is a really difficult one to answer, and we are sure there is no single correct way to go about this. Rather, you need to reflect on your own values when deciding what to do. The first thing to say is that there is a lot of bias in the business world. The second thing to say very quickly is that, for some groups, things are getting a bit better. Bias exists in all forms and its targets include, but are not limited to

- Ethnicity
- Gender
- Sexual preference
- Marital status
- Age
- Health

- Weight
- Height
- Beauty
- Perceived social class
- Address
- Clothes
- Political and religious beliefs
- Education
- Physical disability

Study after study has shown that hiring managers are biased either deliberately or unconsciously, and (guess what!) the most successful job candidates are young, white, attractive, middle-class, well-educated males, followed by their female counterparts.

A recent study we conducted showed that people shown resumes containing photographs of the candidates were more likely to be influenced by the candidate's looks if the candidate was female. For men and women, the less attractive candidates were less likely to be interviewed.

Strategies for dealing with this are very complex and personal. One approach is to conceal information that may prejudice your chances of getting an interview. To some, we know, this can be extremely insulting. They are justifiably proud of themselves and see concealment of facts as playing up to the bigots. This is perfectly understandable, and that is where personal choice comes in.

Health, physical characteristics, age, and marital status are information about yourself we suggest you generally omit. These are irrelevant to most jobs.

If you do decide to conceal your gender or ethnicity on your resume, be sure that you do so consistently. If you have a French-sounding surname such as Depardieu, and you have mentioned that you speak fluent French, you will be assumed to at least be of French descent. If you conceal your gender by using initials rather than first names, stating that you attended Wellesley is a dead giveaway that you're a woman!

Hobbies on your resume can be a giveaway, too (especially if you're branch secretary of the Nebraska Communist Party). It is a sad fact that resumes that conceal some personal details are more likely to be selected for interviews. While we dislike this bias, it is reality, and it is up to you how you deal with it.

If you really wish to include any of the preceding information and are worried about the impact it may have, it probably means you would not be happy working for the organization in question in the first place. It is also worth remembering that, just because the person who reads your resume may be prejudiced, this doesn't mean the people you will work with or for are also prejudiced. People working for recruitment consultants, or people working in human resources departments, may not be anything like the people you'll be working with.

A final point to make here is that generally the bigger the organization, the more likely it is to have Equal Employment Opportunity/Affirmative Action policies and officers. In theory, this should reduce problems of bias.

Gaps in Career History

This is a difficult one, and when we studied several other commercially available resume guides we found that a couple advised that you explain gaps, a couple suggested you conceal gaps, and a couple gave no advice at all!

So we studied the impact of gaps of one year by giving recruiters a series of resumes, some of which had gaps that were explained, some of which had unexplained gaps, and some of which had no gaps. We found the following:

- Recruiters noticed the gaps 50 percent of the time.
- If the gap was noticed and was not explained, recruiters thought the applicant was less honest than the average.
- If the gap was noticed and explained, recruiters thought the applicant was more honest than the average.
- Only one out of ten reasons for a gap ("full-time academic study") was seen as a positive by recruiters.
- Layoffs, both voluntary and involuntary, are still seen poorly by recruiters, despite what some commentators say.
- If the word "caring" (as in "caring for an ill parent") appeared in the explanation of a gap, the recruiters assumed the candidate was female.

Our advice is to explain any gaps—provided you have a good enough story to tell. Remember, the resume is often used at the interview stage to ask candidates questions. If the recruiters do not spot the gap while selecting people to interview, it is likely they will spot it at the interview. If you have had a gap in employment for a very negative reason, such as imprisonment, you may wish to conceal it. However, you must never tell untruths in a resume. Lying about any aspect of your life during recruitment can be grounds for dismissal if uncovered. If you have many unexplained gaps in your work history, then it is almost certain that you should use either the functional resume (see Chapter 8) or the structured interview resume (see Chapter 8). Both of these formats concentrate on skills and abilities and not on dates and times. Think back to the resume see-saw in Chapter 6. These types of resumes emphasize the right side of the see-saw.

What Are the Steps in the Recruitment Process?

There are no hard-and-fast rules about how people recruit, but the steps described below are fairly typical, although some firms will do things in a different order and some organizations will skip certain sections.

Resume Screening

This is what this book is all about! In this stage, employers narrow down the number of applicants by reading their resumes. Sometimes this screening may involve a brief telephone interview with the recruiter or human resources representative before you are asked to submit a resume (and sometimes this telephone screening occurs after the employer has read your resume—there are no hard-and-fast rules about these stages).

Psychological Testing or Assessment

You may be asked to attend an assessment session, which could last between one to five hours (you will be told in advance). You will be asked to complete pencil-and-paper or Web-based tests designed to measure or assess your intelligence, personality, or particular skills such as reading and numeracy.

Interview

The interview stage may consist of one face-to-face interview, or it could involve a whole series of interviews on one day or over a period of time with different people.

A face-to-face interview is the most common and involves you being asked a series of questions about you and your thoughts on the job. Panel interviews have several people at once interviewing you. Do not be nervous—these are often fairer than the face-to-face variety. The questions you are asked here might be prompted by your resume or the results of your psychological testing. Be prepared to explain any gaps on your resume or to describe any aspect of your work history. It is here that liars are easily caught.

Offer or Rejection

About a week to four weeks after the deadline for applications closes, you are likely to hear whether you are being invited for an interview. Unfortunately, employers are often slower to send out rejection letters. You can expect to hear the outcome of an interview a bit more promptly. Often people have arrived home from the interview to find a voice-mail message for them saying "Congratulations!" If you are offered the job, take the time to let things sink in before accepting. Most employers will give you a little time to think things over, but do not expect them to give you very long. Often there is a second choice who they do not wish to lose should you turn them down.

If you are unlucky enough to be rejected, then join the club! You are in the overwhelming majority. Nearly everybody has been turned down for a job at some time or another. If you rejected, do not write a nasty letter or make an abusive phone call to the recruiter or employer—this is highly unprofessional and will risk your reputation with that employer and other prospective employers who hear of your behavior.

Sometimes—and we stress *sometimes*—some employers are willing to provide feedback to you if it is asked for in a polite, positive manner and the purpose is to assist you in strengthening future job applications. However, many employers rightly fear that prolonging the dialogue may expose them to legal action or might mislead the candidate. Sometimes it really is the luck of the draw.

Do I Include References and, If So, Who Should They Be?

There is mixed advice from employers on this topic. Our preference is to include reference contact details as the last item on your resume. The reason for saying this rather than "References available on request" is that it makes it easier for the employer. They do not have to make an extra call to get those names and addresses. If space is tight, you can list full details for three references on a separate sheet. We also wonder how many people who have put "References available on request" have panicked when asked for them because they hadn't bothered to figure out who the references would be! Known to us personally are at least ten examples of candidates who have unwittingly continued to use a reference who has written extremely negative things about them. On other occasions, it is clear that the candidate has failed to ask the permission of a reference in advance when comments such as "Last time I had contact with him he was unemployed in Milwaukee" are made. This brings us to our next golden rule.

➤ **Tip:** Always ensure that you know your references well, and that they are happy to write or say something positive about you.

Not only should you ask the reference's permission, you should treat them with respect. That means you should inform them about the sort of job you are applying for (you don't want a reference to express surprise on the phone). Do not abuse your reference by making them respond to hundreds of different employers that you have indiscriminately applied to.

The best references are people who have supervised you in your recent jobs, especially the one you currently hold. Not only does this look more impressive, it tells the employer that you are not in trouble with your current supervisor. If this is not practical (because you are trying to maintain confidentiality), try using someone who has previously supervised you and has left the company or now works in a different area. Whatever you decide, remember that it is important to have as recent a referee as possible, because this person's comments are most likely to be relevant to the position you are applying for.

If you cannot get a reference from a current or recent employer, or alternatively, the job ad has asked for "character references," you need to approach some other people. This is going to cause outrage among some readers, but there are some people who are more suitable than others to use as character references. In general, people in "professional" jobs are generally seen as "good" references:

- Lawyers
- Judges
- Teachers
- Lecturers
- Police officers
- Government officials
- Company directors (but the company needs to be respectable)
- Senior managers

A Little Reference Levity

Here are a few other horror stories and maybe some urban myths:

- The myth that "the best way of getting rid of a poor employee is to provide them with a brilliant reference" (Companies can now be held liable if they don't warn other companies about potentially dangerous employees.)
- Candidates who serve as their own references
- Candidates who use relatives with different names as references

We have genuinely seen a resume where the candidate had included a statement from a reference who was his best friend's mother—and it was dated more than 14 years before! In another case, a candidate using a false name and address of a reference turned out to be himself using a fake Scottish accent. Unfortunately for him, the accent wore off as the call progressed and he said some unbelievably good things about himself. Needless to say, neither of these applicants got the job!

Do I Include a Photograph?

There are some things we strongly suggest you "conceal," and this especially applies to photographs. Do not include one. Our reasons are these:

- We recently did a survey of a large recruitment firm's archive of resumes and could not find a single successful resume with a photograph attached.
- In another more recent survey we carried out, of more than 625 resumes sent to a recruitment firm, only seven included photographs. Interestingly, six of these candidates were male. There were twice as many males as females, but the males were six times more likely to include a photograph than females. Furthermore, not one of the candidates who attached a photograph was interviewed, compared with 17 percent of the candidates who did not include a photograph.
- Not everyone looks like a supermodel, or photographs like one.
- Sending a photograph is telling employers: "I want to be judged on my looks and not on job-relevant characteristics."
- In a study completed as this book went to press, we compared identical resumes that included a photograph of a person who was independently judged to be attractive or unattractive. The results were depressingly inevitable: Attractive candidates were judged more suitable for the job and were more likely to be interviewed compared to unattractive candidates. This goes for men as well as women. Interestingly, this beauty bias was more evident for women applying for a clerical position than for women applying for a higher-status legal position. We also found that it did not matter whether the job involved seeing clients or customers—attractive candidates were still more highly rated.

What Are Recruiters Thinking When They Read Resumes?

We have extensively researched this question and it is clear that certain themes emerge. Following is a list of comments that have been collected in a series of systematic resume experiments. The comments all come from professional recruitment personnel and human resources officers. We believe these statements give you a unique insight into how recruiters think about the resume screening process. Notice how the comments vary from recruiter to recruiter. Notice also that much of what they are saying is reflected in the advice we have given you in this book. Our advice comes from studies conducted with these professionals and augmented by our professional experience. All the statements in this section are direct quotes taken from interviews and surveys with professional recruiters. The comments refer to resumes we asked the recruiters to read and screen as if they were taking part in a typical recruitment exercise. We asked recruiters about which resumes they liked and why, the problems with the resumes they did not like, and how they came to make their decisions.

What Do Recruiters Like Most in Resumes?

The three factors they appreciated most were:

1. Relevant experience
2. Layout
3. Educational qualifications

Here are five examples of recruiters' comments about resumes they rated highly because of relevant experience:

1. Clear employment history, attributes clearly organized. Resume very well put together and quite clear.
2. Clear, direct description of experience in relation to the competencies described.
3. Computer skills, people skills, experience dealing with managers. A team player, thorough, ambitious.
4. Relevant work experience. Excellent mathematical skills. Strong track record of experience.
5. Scope of experience, ability to work in and coordinate the job unsupervised.

Now see why layout is important in these comments from our team of recruiters:

- Good, clear; layout highlighted awards.
- Clear, well-ordered, logical, easy-to-read. Stable and relevant employment since March '94. Excellent academics.
- Responds to specific needs in the ad. Very well-presented, clearly described details of experience and outcomes.
- Bold headings, logical layouts (qualifications should be on page one). Tasks, duties, position all very clear.
- Highlights those experiences most relevant to the job. Phrasing and format gave strong impression of qualities relevant to the position.

The recruiters responded to resumes emphasizing qualifications in this way:

- Postsecondary education. Work experience relates to job requirements. Business information skills. Relevant extracurricular activities. High level of analysis and motivation. Layout of resume.
- Major assignments and rewards. Length of time employed and duties successfully undertaken while employed. Initiative in having own business.

- College project work (results on paper). Education. Work history. Marketing knowledge.
- Relevant work experience; mix of administration, customer service, analysis. Relevant study/qualifications exposed to systems. Easy to read; well laid out.
- Combination of qualifications, communication skills, expansion on experience, evidence of drive, energy, appropriate focus and experience.

What Do Recruiters Dislike in a Resume?

Here are five examples of comments made by recruiters about resumes they did not like, starting with relevant experience:

1. Very little experience (in time spent); too theoretical, that is, skills are demonstrated in education, not in work. College results (although comprehensive) show weaknesses in areas of most importance.
2. Previous employment history does not exactly mix with the job being applied for.
3. Academic, little experience. Lacks ambition and enthusiasm; no continuity of employment.
4. Not as much relevant experience, although shows initiative through own business. Layout of resume a little difficult to read.
5. Mainly research experience. Concerns about how applicant would do in the real world.

Poor layout can leave a poor impression on recruiters and employers, as these examples show:

1. Layout of resume terrible. Information too difficult to make sense of.
2. Format annoying. Information irrelevant to this job.
3. Resume all over the place. No logic; difficult to follow. I can't be bothered persevering to find information.
4. Little reference to position description. Poor point size. Bad layout with two columns. Very busy resume.
5. Too much information per page. No logical sequence. Text is very small, although information is very good.

Recruiters looking for qualifications react very negatively when they're not there. For example:

- No demonstration or examples of the required/desired competencies. Nothing outstanding that would lead to thinking there may be special qualities.
- Does not show academic details. Poor detail on positions held.

- Job advertisement is looking for someone with a strong desire to pursue a sales career. This applicant has been "behind the scenes."
- Limited experience while working in buying field. Comparing resumes, this one has the least experience (in college and work).
- Leaves me with the feeling that I need to be informed of more detail to appropriately gauge the candidate's suitability.

How Do Recruiters Use Job Competencies to Discern a Good "Fit"?

In a recent study, we looked at the effectiveness of including competency statements on resumes. Taking a sales analyst's position as an example, we asked a team of professional recruiters to list, in order of importance, the 10 competencies they most valued and comment on them. We then counted the number of times all the recruiters mentioned those competencies in their comments.

The results, shown in Table 16.1, reflect that count and show the competencies the recruiters regarded as important for the position of sales analyst. (If we carried out this exercise for a different position—for example, a laboratory technician— the results would be very different.) As you can see, an overall pattern emerges suggesting that communication skills and numerical skills were regarded as the most important. This supports the idea that recruiters build up their own opinions of which competencies are ideal for a particular position—in this case a sales analyst.

Table 16.1: Effectiveness of Competency Statements

Competency	Number of Times Mentioned
Communication skills	31
Numerical skills	26
Planning and organizing	20
Market knowledge	19
Achievement orientation	17
Initiative with responsibility	16
Problem solving	11
Motivation	11
Energy	6
Tenacity	3

Table 16.2 provides some samples of why the different recruiters thought the different competencies were important for the sales analyst position.

Table 16.2: Comments on Most-Valued Competencies

Most-Valued Competencies	Recruiter's Comments
Achievement orientation	This is needed to keep up the level of motivation and move from an analysis role to a sales-oriented role in the future. Applicant needs to be an achiever with an understanding of the business, driven to assist Account Managers.
Achievement orientation with communication skills	Any sales role needs a track record of demonstrable success. Communication skills are critical in sales.
Achievement orientation with initiative and responsibility	The applicant needs drive, ability, and tenacity to meet goals. A new graduate should be questioned about the responsibility to undertake activities and see them through.
Achievement orientation with numerical skills	This new position depends on achieving results in increased sales/market share. Key technical skill is the ability to collect and process relevant data. If this was not applicable, then communication skills would be ranked highest. This sales analyst role is to provide crucial information to assist in final sales. It requires extensive analysis.
Achievement orientation with planning and organizing skills	The successful candidate must be goal oriented to handle this position, which will need planning and organizing skills because it is a new role.

continued

continued

Most-Valued Competencies	Recruiter's Comments
Communication skills	This is the most valued competency because you can achieve anything with good communicators. There is internal and external liaison involved. Analysts need to get their conclusion across to their managers as well as clients. Customers demand excellent communication skills and a commitment to deliver.
Communication skills with initiative and responsibility	Written, oral and listening skills form the key to succeeding in this job. The position needs a person who will work diligently without constant supervision.
Communication skills with market knowledge	This role requires collective market /product information and collating in a form that can be used by clients. Experience in a team environment is required to deal with many parties, and to distribute information. It's clearly important for the applicant to have some idea of, and background in, the market area involved.
Communication with problem-solving skills	The concerns of customers will always need a high level of problem solving.
Communication with numerical skills	Ability to communicate with a wide range of people, know how the industry operates, and interpret requirements for analysis are imperative.

continued

continued

Most-Valued Competencies	Recruiter's Comments
Communication with planning and organizing skills	Verbal ability to liaise with customers/peers/managers is essential. Excellent written communication required in user-friendly presentation of data/results. Applicant will need to be a self-starter who is able to plan and organize own schedule.
Energy	Customer and account manager service will be directly affected by the energy and "urgency" of the person who fills this role.
Initiative with responsibility	The job needs a person who takes their workload seriously and responsibly and creates efficiency through reduced human resource management. The applicant must be able to take on responsibility, empower people, and be able to take knocks and bounce back.
Initiative with responsibility and achievement orientation	Initiative and responsibility need to be established as priorities; otherwise, all else is affected. Respect, awareness, and commitment are paramount, particularly within a team environment.
Initiative with responsibility and problem-solving skills	Because the job reports to several managers, the applicant needs to be a self starter. The role is analytically focused with the need to collect data and work through it piece by piece, as well as see the big picture, to get results.

continued

continued

Most-Valued Competencies	Recruiter's Comments
Initiative with responsibility and tenacity	This person needs less direction, and will produce a higher work output of greater quality than others.
Market knowledge	The ability to monitor products from their own and a competitive situation is essential to the business performance. Important to understand what the products are and where they fit in the marketplace.
Market knowledge with communication skills	Proof of efforts to understand and research market areas is essential. Manner is as important as ability and aptitude.
Market knowledge with planning and organizing	The role requires a good understanding of the market to perform the job to the best ability.
Motivation	Enthusiasm will allow even the least competent to shine.
Motivation with energy	These competencies are by far the most important. Without them, you will only ever be employed as an assistant sales analyst. These competencies are far in excess of the need for the candidate to be a graduate.
Motivation with initiative and responsibility	To provide constant and accurate reports to both customers and colleagues.
Numerical skills	You can't analyze if you can't do the math. The role involves evaluation of sales forecasts versus actuals. Without good numerical analysis skills in this area, the business could lose sales.

continued

continued

Most-Valued Competencies	Recruiter's Comments
Numerical skills with communication	The role requires numerical reasoning and understanding; liaison with account managers, marketplace providers, and users has to be clear and concise. This role includes analysis of data, sales forecasts, and monitoring pricing as well as liaison, report preparation, and promotion strategies.
Planning and organizing	The applicant needs good skills in this area to cope with the volume and variety of work, and juggle the number of people to report to.
Planning and organizing with communication skills	Given the number of projects involved in this role and account manager liaison, the ability to plan and organize oneself is critical. The need to liaise with customers, gather information, and determine their needs makes communication skills critical.
Planning and organizing with numerical skills	The role involves organizing and planning data collection and collation. Statistical skills in analyzing results are essential. There are many reports and analytical work required on sales and marketing issues.
Planning and organizing with problem-solving skills	This competency requires an ability to collate and deliver information to others; a need to ascertain and analyze data and evaluate various information.

continued

continued

Most-Valued Competencies	Recruiter's Comments
Problem solving	Good problem-solving skills are necessary to support the numerical skills in evaluating and reporting market information. The role requires exceptional analytical ability.
Tenacity	People with tenacity are more likely to succeed than people who rely on any other individual competency.

In contrast to the information given on the previous pages, we asked recruiters to list which of 10 different competencies was their least valued when recruiting somebody into the position of a sales analyst. And again, we counted the number of times they mentioned those competencies.

Table 16.3: Frequency of Competencies Mentioned

Competency	Number of Times Mentioned
Tenacity	34
Energy	33
Motivation	18
Market knowledge	9
Numerical skills	9
Problem-solving	7
Initiative with responsibility	5
Achievement orientation	3
Communication skills	3
Planning and organizing	1

Tenacity and energy were the least-valued competencies, followed by motivation. As with the most-valued competencies, there is strong opinion among the recruiters about the competencies that are not so important when preparing a resume for the sales analyst position. Table 16.4 provides samples of the recruiters' comments about why they considered the various competencies to be of little value.

Table 16.4: Comments on Least-Valued Competencies

Least-Valued Competencies	Recruiters' Comments
Achievement orientation	It is a back-office role and tends to be fairly process oriented. Someone with a strong achievement orientation could become bored. This job does not require someone dominant in nature, as long as the job gets done within the time frame.
Communication skills	Person needs only to communicate internally at this stage, with no client contact.
Energy	Energy is good but knowledge and efficiency are more important.
Initiative with responsibility	The applicants do not need as much of this because the position is a junior role.
Market knowledge	This can be learned within months on the job. This is an entry-level position and market knowledge would not be needed at this point.
Motivation	It is hard to tell this competency from resumes. It is needed but is not as important if goals are achieved. This person may be in the job for some time before promotion.

continued

continued

Least-Valued Competencies	Recruiters' Comments
Numerical skills	All candidates should have this skill, but other competencies rank more highly because part of the position relates to personal and other skills.
Planning and organizing	The person will report to line managers, so his or her responsibilities will be structured.
Problem-solving	Because the role is predominantly about producing reports from available data, this is not so important. The person would be under the wing of the sales manager and could develop this skill over time.
Tenacity	The position has been created to support the sales team. The candidates should not have to sell their services. Tenacity is useless when gathering information.

What Do Recruiters Think About When They Make Decisions on Resumes?

We asked two recruiters to think out loud when reading resumes. We recorded their thoughts on each, and then grouped them according to the recruiter's decision.

Recruiter 1

Decision	Comments
Resume rejected	• The resume includes mistaken terminology for "customers."

continued

continued

Decision	Comments
	• It is reasonably articulate but the applicant's grammar and communication skills are questionable.
	• The letter is too long. It taps into a few things about the role advertised, but focuses on marketing, not sales.
	• The applicant has an associate diploma instead of the necessary degree.
	• The applicant describes skills but the ad says the employer wants a demonstrated track record of achievement.
Unsure of resume at this stage	• It's too short and includes the applicant's marital status, which is irrelevant and annoying.
	• I question their expectations, but I like the cover letter.
	• I'm not into what they think they're good at. I'd prefer to see what they have done.
	• I need to know how much business experience the applicant has had.
Interview granted, based on resume	• The candidate is able to demonstrate achievement.
	• The candidate worked all the way through college.
	• The resume demonstrates that the candidate can manage a number of tasks.
	• The candidate lists financial forecasting, statistics, and computer literacy.
	• It was an average resume, but the candidate has a good academic record.

Recruiter 2

Decision	Comments
Resume rejected	• The resume is very hard to read. • There is too much high-school education. The college section is better laid out. • The only interesting thing in the resume is that the candidate speaks Japanese. • There is nothing to support the candidate's original claims. • The candidate includes too much detail about extracurricular activities.
Unsure of resume at this stage	• The letter is quite interesting. The candidate starts off by saying what he or she does now and how he or she might relate to this job. • The candidate has retail experience, but the position doesn't need this. • Computer skills are important and the resume is well laid out. • The format of the resume is easy to scan.
Interview granted, based on resume	• In terms of key criteria, the competencies listed on the resume include achievement orientation and cooperation. • The interesting format makes me interested in the candidate. • Putting the candidate's attributes up front is a good idea.

How Do Recruiters Decide Which Candidates to Interview?

We asked recruiters to list the most common strategies they used in selecting candidates for interviews. Here are some of their answers.

Table 16.5: Recruiters' Strategies

1. The quality of written words and the structure of the cover letter.
2. Relevant experience.
3. Evidence of activities that indicate the nature of the applicant.

---

1. Academic qualifications are reviewed first, followed by a scan of the resume.
2. The structure of the cover letter is very important. Spelling mistakes are frowned upon.
3. Attention is focused on recent work experience.

---

1. Look for experience that approximates what is required.

---

1. Match candidate's competencies with the position.
2. Match work experience with the position.
3. Check the candidate's post-secondary education.

---

1. Compare the candidate's experience and qualifications with their competencies.

---

1. Read the resume thoroughly.
2. Review the competencies.
3. Consider how the resume matches the competencies.
4. Reevaluate the resume.
5. Make a decision on whether to reject it or recommend an interview.

---

1. The candidate's knowledge, experience, and personal traits are compared with those required for the position.

---

1. Read the cover letter to evaluate the standard of writing and the ability to address advertisement requests.
2. Then scan the resume to check whether education and experience requirements are met before reading the resume in depth to gauge the candidate's level of achievement, responsibility, team involvement, etc.

---

1. Qualifications, experience.
2. Evidence of literacy, expression, numeracy.
3. Potential, apparent focus.

Do Recruiters Eliminate Resumes on One Piece of Information?

Here are a few sample responses from our recruiters:

- Yes. I eliminated one candidate because he had a poor cover letter and errors in the resume. This indicates lack of attention to detail and care.
- Yes, because of spelling errors and poor grammar.
- I look to include applicants rather than to eliminate them, but I finally rank and select the strongest candidates.
- No, never.
- I am definitely put off by typos, spelling and grammar errors. If you can't get it right when you're trying to make a good impression, what about every day?
- Not really; it is a matter of one resume not being as good as another resume.
- I look for the amount of information around achievements.
- If a degree does not include a relevant major, I query real interest in the job and ability to perform. This combined with very limited experience in the area means they would not be considered for interview.
- No. At least a couple of factors worked together.

Our Professional Recruiters Tell You Their Best Tips

Each recruiter was asked to nominate a single piece of advice for writers of resumes. Here are their comments:

- Make sure you have correct grammar with no spelling errors in the cover letter and address the competencies required in the advertisement.
- The resume should contain a clear, concise, and chronological format.
- Highlight the skills that meet the criteria and market, and write with a positive attitude.
- Remember that you are marketing yourself, so while the integrity of the document is a must, the resume needs to present your best qualities and must detail your relevant skills and competencies.
- Include specifics like "I achieved a 30 percent increase in sales through the telesales initiative I introduced."
- Do not overstate facts in the cover letter that can be obtained from reading the resume.

- Keep your resume short and to-the-point.
- Tailor the resume to suit the requirements of the ad and include achievements, not just duties, because these are what will sell you.
- Include examples to back up your competency statements.
- Follow my 4-S rule: Keep your resume "Simple, Structured, Succinct, and Significant."
- Make sure your resume supports the advertised position criteria and the feel of the ad without waffling.
- Use a sharp cover letter and restrict the resume to two pages. Identify your strengths and weaknesses, if possible. Emphasize aspects of your background that have an immediate or apparent match with the job requirements.
- Put your major achievements and accomplishments in the resume, not just tasks and responsibilities.
- Avoid being repetitive in your resume.
- Use the active voice to describe what you have done in previous positions, and say why you want the job.
- Do your homework prior to applying. Find out about the company; obtain an annual report if available; find out what future projects the company might be involved with, who their clients are, and who their competitors are.
- Clearly address the specific requirements called for so that the skills can be easily measured against the criteria, and then against those of the other applicants.
- Provide as much information as possible on work experience and post-secondary education.

Using Your Resume on the Internet

> > > > > > > > > > > *In the last part* of this book, we have provided you with some valuable resources to assist you in your resume preparation and job seeking. Increasingly, job seeking is being conducted via the Internet, so we have provided you with some useful links. Given the nature of the Internet, some of these inevitably will change in one way or another by the time you read this. However, we trust there will be enough useful sites to get your Net surfing started!

CHAPTER 17

Getting Your Resume Online

The development in electronic communications has brought about many new possibilities. We can now advertise jobs on the Internet, apply for jobs on the Internet, submit our resumes to sites on the Internet, e-mail our resumes directly to employers, and set up personal Web pages on the Internet. Recruiters can now electronically scan resumes, in order to do all the screening automatically. Yes, it is now possible that only a computer will read your resume! Finally, many more people now have access to word processors—which brings its own problems.

Creating Electronic Resumes

This section discusses the ins and outs of the various different types of electronic resumes: scannable, e-mailed, PDF, and Web resumes.

Tips for Resumes That Will Be Scanned

All scanners work on the same principles. They are looking for keywords or phrases that have been programmed into the computer. The words that companies scan for are often nouns and proper nouns—for instance, "Excel," "Word," or "automatic payroll systems." If you think it likely that your resume will be scanned electronically, this may be the time to use jargon or specialist language—provided that it is meaningful to people in your own industry. So you can use terms like

- AI (artificial intelligence)
- SPSS (a computer program)
- ROI (return on investment)
- WYSIWYG (what you see is what you get)

➤ **Tip:** Use lots of relevant nouns and proper nouns on your resume to increase the chances that scanners will pick them up.

Format is also important for scanned resumes. Layout should be clear and easy for a scanner to read. The use of headings can assist here—remember, where you might otherwise refrain from using a heading for fear of insulting your reader's intelligence, computers do not have feelings, so spell everything out for them! Headings such as the following may be useful:

- Experience
- Education
- Qualifications
- Work History
- Affiliations
- References

The computer programs used to read your resume are becoming increasingly sophisticated, and therefore it is a canny idea to use some keywords to describe your personal qualities here, too. Look back at the typical qualities that companies look for and, of course, the ones you have deduced from your detective work. Words that might be useful here are

- Leader or leadership
- Communicator
- Dynamic
- Energetic
- Excellent
- Outstanding
- Skilled
- Intelligent
- Team player
- Team-focused
- Outgoing
- Persuasive
- Dependable
- Reliable

Unusual fonts are never a good idea, especially when the resume might be scanned. Use Times, Times New Roman, Optima, Arial, Palatino, or Courier. The font size should be in the normal letter range of 10 to 14 points. Although earlier we suggested that a 16-point font for your name looks good, err on the side of caution if you think the resume is going to be scanned and use a smaller font. If you include telephone numbers, list each one on a separate line, as a scanner may read numbers on the same line as one number. This will cause difficulties for people who subsequently look you up in a computer database when they want to contact you. Underlining can make scanning more difficult, and doesn't look appealing generally, so desist.

The layout also affects the number of characters per line. In general, you should ensure that you do not have more than 70 to 80 characters per line, or scanning programs may reproduce the resume with some lines wrapped around to the next line, causing the formatting to be messed up.

Avoid using columns like a newspaper. Start each new piece of information on a new line, fully aligned to the left. Look back to Chapter 9, where we compare different layouts. The best layout for a machine-readable resume is Resume 1.

Do not put lines, pictures, or graphics on your resume, as these will confuse the scanner.

Finally, if you are mailing your resume to the employer using conventional mail, try to avoid folding it up to put it in an envelope. Put the resume in an appropriately sized envelope, preferably one that has a reinforced cardboard back to help prevent creasing.

E-mailing Resumes

As an alternative to mailing your resume, some employers are now happy to receive them electronically via e-mail. This can speed up the hiring process and can save money, too. If you are applying for a job that requires some IT knowledge, sending your resume by e-mail will demonstrate that you are comfortable with this type of technology. However, there are a few points to take into consideration.

As with scanned resumes, you should keep to a maximum of 70 to 80 characters per line. Any more and you risk losing the formatting. You should send the resume as an attachment. Do not be tempted to copy and paste it into the body of the e-mail—you will lose most of the formatting. Remember, even though you may have a fancy e-mail program that allows you to include formatting and graphics in the message body, the majority of e-mail programs do not allow this, and all you will do is send an unintelligible mess to your prospective employer.

There are two further options you might want to consider. The first is to paste a text version of your resume into the body of the e-mail. Some people advise you to do this because some recruiters may worry about opening attachments to e-mails for fear of any viruses they contain. The pros of this are that you get your information to the recruiter. The downside is that we know that the visual appeal of the resume has a dramatic effect on the recruiter, and this type of resume is not visually appealing. Second, some employers who might be happy to open attachments might overlook the attachment if they see the resume included in the body of the e-mail, and will work from the impoverished version of your work of art!

Our recommendation is only do this as a last resort. If you are organized, you will have time in advance of the deadline to contact the recruiter by phone or e-mail and ask whether they will accept an attachment.

The second strategy is to save your resume as an Adobe Acrobat PDF file. Adobe Acrobat is a program that converts word processor and graphics files into a file that preserves the exact look of the document regardless of what computer is used to open the document. This will get you over all of the formatting and template issues associated with sending traditional word processor files such as Microsoft Word or WordPerfect. It also demonstrates that you are computer literate.

In order to save your file in the "PDF" format, you will need special software, or will need to check whether your word processor has a "save as" option to save files to PDF format. Specialized software to save files to the PDF format is available for download on the Net, for modest cost (for example, edoc Printer PDF Pro is about $30).

If you do decide to attach the resume as a file, you need to consider carefully what word-processing program you are going to use to generate the resume and, just as importantly, what version of the program you are going to use. Many large-scale commercial companies hold back from buying the very latest version of a piece of software because of cost, and to ensure that the new version is bug free. Often the job ad will specify which programs are acceptable and which are not. If there are no guidelines, phone the company and ask. If this is not possible, the safest bet is to send a PC-compatible file (not a Mac file), saved as Microsoft Word, Version 6 for Windows 95. It is a slightly older version, which means most people should be able to read it. Another safe bet is to save and send the file as "text only," but you will lose all your formatting by doing this, and you have to ask whether you are losing more than you are gaining by sending your resume by e-mail.

Resumes sent electronically may not be as secure as those sent by conventional mail. If your application is very sensitive, this point needs considering. Many companies now routinely monitor their employees' e-mail and net usage, making this a less confidential medium. One solution is to get your own e-mail account. Many companies offer these free of charge. Alternatively, you could visit an Internet cafe or your local public library. They will often provide a suitable service and may be able to assist you if you are unsure how the e-mail process works.

E-mail is an easy and quick way to send things, but resist the temptation to compose your resume and mail it off immediately. Many of us have had that sinking feeling just after we have hit the send button that we have sent the wrong version, sent it to the wrong person, or have just realized it contains a glaring error.

➤ **Tip:** Always print a copy of your resume and have someone else read it before mailing or e-mailing it.

Web Page Resumes

Another innovation is the Web page as a resume. These fall into two categories: individuals who build a personal Web page and bring it to the employer's attention; and companies that allow you to enter your details either into their standard resume form or by cutting and pasting your file on to their site. The resume is then indexed and stored on their site for future employers to search through.

Personal Web pages demonstrate the remarkable things that people will reveal about themselves that they'd never dream of including in a professional document! Employers are generally not interested in "meeting the babies," "looking at my boat," or "seeing my front room." If you intend to set up your Web page as a substitute resume, you must apply the same level of professionalism that you would to a conventional resume. The key difference with a Web page resume is that you can include far more information, provided that it is appropriately indexed and the site is easily navigable. However, the initial key pages of the site should convey all the critical information of a conventional resume. Use the extra potential of a Web site for additional optional information in links that employers can choose to follow.

Keep in mind that Web site resumes become public documents, which potentially can be accessed by anyone, including your current boss. Do you really want all your personal details laid out for everyone to see?

There are hundreds, maybe thousands, of different job Web sites, and many of these allow you to post an online resume. So, which Web sites should you put your resume on, and how do you go about it? This chapter gives you the lowdown on the most popular sites and gives a step-by-step example of how to put your resume on one site.

Ways of Posting Your Resume

There are generally two ways to get your resume into an online resume bank. You can either upload your current resume, or you can build one from scratch using the forms on the site.

Attaching an Existing Resume

Some sites allow you to upload a copy of your resume to their site so that employers can search it. To do this, you will need to have your resume saved on the computer you are using or on a floppy disk, CD, or other removable storage device. Then follow the instructions on the screen to attach your resume. The resume should have a simple title like "resume.doc" (unless the site directs you to do otherwise) and be saved in a common format such as .doc, .txt, .rtf, .htm, .html, .wpd, .pdf, .ppt, or .xls.

Monster.com is a Web site that allows you to attach a resume in response to some of its job advertisements. At the top of the ad it will say "Apply Now." Click on this and follow the instructions.

➤ **Tip:** Take the time to review any resume that has been previously unsuccessful before resubmitting it, just in case you could make some adjustments that might result in you being chosen for an interview.

Let's have a look at how you might go about creating a resume on Monster.

Creating a Resume on Monster.com

The Web site www.monster.com and other Web sites enable you to create an online resume. Here is a guide to doing this.

1. Go to the Monster home page by typing www.monster.com.
2. Click the Post your Resume button (circled for you).
3. Next, you will have to register with Monster (if you are not already registered).
4. To register, you click on the "Continue" button and then fill out the registration form.
5. There is some more information required, but the end of the form contains an important question about how you want to submit your resume. You have the option to use Monster's resume builder, which will take you through a step-by-step process to getting all of your information together.
6. Alternatively, you can use a Microsoft Word resume, copy and paste a plain-text resume, have one written by an expert, or create your resume later. If you have followed the steps in this book, there is no doubt your best option is to attach your Microsoft Word resume. If you want a resume written by an expert, contact us (brightandassociates.com.au) and we'll do it for you!
7. After you have finished your registration, go back to the home page and click on "attach an existing resume."
8. The next thing you have to do is enter a 70-character (maximum) "Resume Headline" (snappy title) to attract an employer's attention. Think carefully about what to put here. Some examples are given on the form.

Here are some more:

Outstanding Sales Representative

High Achieving Claypot Maker

Attention-Detailed Ocularist

Dynamic Chicken Sexer

Always compose your Resume Headline in MS Word first and then cut and paste it into the space provided on the form. This way, you can double-check that you haven't exceeded the character length (use the word-count feature in Word for this). Also, you can spell-check your headline.

9. Then use the Browse button to search your computer's hard disk to locate the resume you want to upload. (Hint: Make sure that you have saved your resume with a really unambiguous name to ensure that you do not get confused and upload Aunty Throttlepuss's draft resume by mistake!)

10. Follow the instructions and save the resume. Hey, presto! You have your resume on the Web, and now you can finish helping your Aunty Throttlepuss get a position as a Marine Assault Librarian.

Internet Sites for Job Seekers

The Internet is a great tool to search for jobs, post your resume, get some career tips, and find out more about the companies you are interested in applying to. We debated about providing Web addresses because, as with all things on the Web, sites change and come and go so rapidly, we cannot vouch for all these sites or their content. Please accept our apologies in advance if any of the information has changed. Most useful are the sites held by the big search engines (see AltaVista Careers or Excite Careers, for example). These have useful links to other related sites. To search the Web for yourself, use terms such as "jobs" + "resume bank."

Job Hunting Web Sites

For some resources to help you in your job and advertisement research, check out the following sites, which have been put together with the assistance of Lene Jensen and her team at the University of New South Wales Careers and Employment Service.

Company Name	Web Site Address	Nature
Academic 360	www.academic360.com	For the academic job finder.
Academic Employment Network	www.academploy.com	Lists educational job vacancies.

continued

continued

Company Name	Web Site Address	Nature
After College	www.thejobresource.com	Specializes in job search and people search for post-graduates.
America's Job Bank	www.ajb.dni.us	U.S. government-sponsored job search site.
Benefit Links	www.benefitslink.com	Compliance information and special search tools.
Best Jobs USA	www.bestjobsusa.com	Connects employers to qualified professionals.
Career Babe	www.careerbabe.com	Specializes in job searching for college students, school students, and libraries.
Career Builder	www.careerbuilder.com	Jobs search and job alerts.
Career Exchange USA—Category	www.careerexchange.com	Search by job category.
Career Exchange USA—Location	www.careerexchange.com	Search by job location.
Career Journal	www.careerjournal.com	From the *Wall Street Journal* Web site.
Career Magazine	www.careermag.com	Job search for all types of employment.
Career Site	www.career.com	Resume writing services and job searching.
Career Tips	www.careertips.com/usa	Large network of jobs and job hunting resources.

continued

continued

Company Name	Web Site Address	Nature
Careers	www.jsu.edu	Job finding links.
Careers in Art Librarianship	www.arlisna.org/careers	Help finding careers in art librarianship and visual resources.
College Grad	www.collegegrad.com	Specializes in college graduate job searching.
Employment Guide.com	www.employmentguide.com	Large job search Web site.
Help Wanted	www.helpwanted.net	Large network of jobs and job hunting resources.
Hot Jobs	www.hotjobs.yahoo.com	Job search for all types of employment.
IMDiversity	www.imdiversity.com	Equal-opportunity job search site.
Internship Programs	www.internships.wetfeet.com	Search for internships.
Job Accommodation Network	www.jan.wvu.edu	Educational site providing job search links.
Job Bank USA	www.jobbankusa.com	U.S.-only job search site.
Job Find	www.jobfind.com	Job search for all types of employment.
Job Finder	www.jobfinder.com	Job search for all types of employment.
Job Hunt	www.job-hunt.org	Access to available jobs and job hunting resources.
Job Match	www.redirector.monster.com	Cincinnati job matching service.
Job Net	www.job.net	Help finding jobs by location.

continued

continued

Company Name	Web Site Address	Nature
Job Network	www.jobnet.com	Large network of jobs and job hunting resources.
Job Star	www.jobstar.org	International job search site.
Job.com	www.job.com	Post your resume and search.
Job.Net	www.job-net.com	Job search for the North and South Carolina area.
Management Recruiters International	www.mrinetwork.com	Mid- to senior-level employment search.
MAXIMUS	www.maximus.com	Government career counseling organization.
Mega Job Site	www.megajobsite.com	Job searching and links to other job network providers.
Monster	www.monster.com	A must to visit.
MonsterTRAK	www.monstertrak.com	Specializes in college graduate job searching.
My Future	www.myfuture.com	Specializes in job search and people search for post-graduates.
Nation Job	www.nationjob.com	U.S.-only job search site.
Net Temps	www.nettemps.com	Specializes in freelance and temp jobs.
Nursing Options USA	www.nursingoptions.com	Source for registered nurses and nursing management.

continued

continued

Company Name	Web Site Address	Nature
Occupational Outlook Handbook	www.bls.gov	A guide to occupations.
Opportunity Knocks	www.opportunitynocs.org	Non-profit career opportunities.
The Riley Guide	www.rileyguide.com	Job search for all types of employment.
Rite Site	www.ritesite.com	Executive job search site.
U.S. Department of Labor's Career Guide to Industries	www.bls.gov/oco/cg	Information about America's top industries.
Vault	www.vault.com	Specializes in post-graduates.
Voip Tools	www.voipproviderslist.com	Job searching and links to other job network providers.
Yahoo! HotJobs	hotjobs.yahoo.com	Top job search site.

Search Terms

URLs are subject to change, so don't bank on going back to your "Favorites" list as always the best way to identify vacancies. You might try experimenting with search terms in a large search engine, such as Google, using the terms "job vacancies," to generate a list of the larger sites. Remember to look at the headers and sidebars (many of the larger sites will advertise here in response to your search). Also visit professional associations of which you are a member or are eligible for membership in. Many of these will have links to job vacancies or employers will advertise on the association's Web site.

Index

X–Z